What Makes It Great?

Short Masterpieces, Great Composers

ROB KAPILOW

Lincoln Center

WILEY

John Wiley & Sons, Inc.

Lincoln Center and Lincoln Center for the Performing Arts names and logos are registered trademarks of Lincoln Center for the Performing Arts, Inc., in the United States and other countries. Used here by license.

Recordings for accompanying website and enhanced e-books provided by Naxos of America, with the exception of chapter 2 (Bach), which was provided by Konstantin Soukhovetski (piano).

Published by John Wiley & Sons, Inc., Hoboken, New Jersey
Published simultaneously in Canada

Design and composition by Forty-Five Degree Design, LLC

For general information about our other products and services, please contact our Customer Care Department within the United States at (800) 762-2974, outside the United States at (317) 572-3993 or fax (317) 572-4002.

Wiley also publishes its books in a variety of electronic formats. Some content that appears in print may not be available in electronic books. For more information about Wiley products, visit our web site at www.wiley.com.

Library of Congress Cataloging-in-Publication Data:
Kapilow, Robert.
    What makes it great? : short masterpieces, great composers / by Rob Kapilow.
        p. cm.
    Includes bibliographical references and index.
    ISBN 978-0-470-55092-2 (cloth); ISBN 978-1-118-05814-5 (ebk);
ISBN 978-1-118-05815-2 (ebk); ISBN 978-1-118-05816-9 (ebk);
ISBN 978-1-118-17198-1 (ebk); ISBN 978-1-118-17199-8 (ebk)
    1. Music preparation. I. Title.
    MT6.K234W43 2011
    781.1'7—dc23   2011018342

Printed in the United States of America
10 9 8 7 6 5 4 3 2 1

CONTENTS

ACKNOWLEDGMENTS

It is one thing to delude yourself into believing that you might have something of value to say in a single book. It is quite something else to believe you actually have enough to say to merit a second one. For this delusion, I would like to cheerfully thank my editor/saint at Wiley for both books, Hana Lane; my literary agent, Carl Brandt; and my manager, Charles Letourneau at IMG. In addition, I would like to thank Lincoln Center for their continued support of this second book and Naxos Records, which provided the recordings for the book's musical examples—with particular thanks to Randall Foster, who helped to make this possible. I also cannot give enough credit to my two superb assistants from Juilliard, Nicholas Csicsko and Sasha Popov, who once again undertook the daunting task of making the book's musical examples spring to life both on the page and on the website. Without their dedication, perseverance, and painstaking work, this book would not have been possible.

I would also like to thank my wife and children, who put up with me as I fought my way through the writing of the book, and in particular my son Benjamin, who read nearly all of the manuscript and offered the kind of brutal if valuable criticism that could come only from a budding teenage composer.

Finally, I would like to thank the many readers of my first book who were kind enough to write to me and let me know how much the book enriched their listening. Their enthusiasm and excitement helped convince me that I was on the right path and encouraged me to continue the conversation in this second book.

HOW TO USE THE WEBSITE

To complement the text of this book, we have created a website where you can see and listen to the musical examples used in this book. Watch the scroll bar move along with the notes as they're played, or download the .mp4 files to your computer.

To listen to or download the files, follow these steps:

1. Enter www.wiley.com/go/whatmakesitgreat into your Internet browser.
2. Click on the chapter you are looking for in the list located on the left side of the page *or* click on the link labeled "Download All Examples" to save all the examples to a location of your choice on your computer.
3. Click on the numbered example you want to listen to.

If you want to download the files to an .mp4-compatible portable device, such as an iPod, follow your portable device's directions on downloading an .mp4 file.

That's all there is to it. Have fun, and remember, all you have to do is listen.

> Also look for the new enhanced e-book edition, which incorporates the musical examples from the website into the text. It is available for devices that support enhanced e-books and video playback.

[INTRODUCTION]

"To Know One Thing Well"

If you watch people walk down the street playing a pop song on their iPods or drive by in a car blasting the latest chart-topping rap song at full volume, you cannot help but be struck by the intensely engaged way they listen. They react physically to every beat of the music and invariably sing along or move their mouths to every word of a vocal line that they have effortlessly memorized through repeated hearings on their radio or playlist. Even after twenty years have gone by, most people can still remember the pop songs of their teenage years word for word, note for note, and frequently, according to researcher Dan Levitin, in their original key. Aaron Copland said that you don't really "own" a piece of music until you can sing it through in your head from beginning to end, and a song doesn't really arrive on the popular landscape until fans everywhere know by heart not only every word and note of the vocal line, but every rhythm and gesture of the accompaniment as well.

Because ideas and forms in popular music are generally short and repetitive, and because people tend to listen to current hits over and over again, learning to sing a popular song in one's head from beginning to end takes little effort. However, singing a complex, fifty-minute Beethoven symphony in one's head from beginning to end, even after repeated hearings, is far more challenging. In general, performers, as a group, tend to find it easier to meet Copland's ownership requirement

1

than do nonperformers. Anyone who has ever played an instrument, sung in a chorus, played chamber music, or been part of a band or an orchestra knows that over time, practicing and rehearsing a piece of music bit by bit almost invariably produces the ability to sing it through in their head from beginning to end. But what about the music lover who does not play an instrument or read music—one of the key groups this book is written for? Can a nonmusician own a piece of classical music like a performer or a pop-music listener?

I hope that this book answers that question with a resounding yes. One of the central goals of this book is to help you own eighteen short masterpieces by eighteen great composers. Like a performer, we will learn these pieces slowly; measure by measure, phrase by phrase, and layer by layer, so that by the time you finish the book, you will not only be able to sing these pieces through in your head from beginning to end but will also have a rich, in-depth understanding of their language and style. Each chapter will focus on the achievement of one major composer by looking extremely closely at one short masterpiece from his body of work—either a complete piece like an aria, a prelude, or a song, or an individual movement from a larger work, like a sonata or a quartet. To facilitate ownership, I have chosen the shortest pieces I could find that effectively convey the central features of each composer's style. In each chapter, after briefly establishing a conceptual/historical context for each composer and piece, I will offer a close examination of one short work as a window on that composer's genius. I will discuss each piece from three continually overlapping points of view. First and foremost, how is the piece put together, and what makes it great? Second, in what way is the piece a representative example of the core achievement of that particular composer? How does the piece exemplify Beethoven's or Bach's style? Finally, in what way does the piece work with and transform the musical language of its time?

It is my deepest belief that what is great about these pieces is gettable by both musicians and nonmusicians alike, and I hope that this book will be valuable to a wide range of listeners, from first-time concertgoers to trained musicians. New, innovative, user-friendly technology is at the heart of this book, and this technology is the key to my attempt to address nonmusicians in an engaging, in-depth way. To write about music in any kind of meaningful detail requires that the reader be able to hear the music you are describing. Though a trained musician might be capable of looking at musical notation in a book and hearing the sound in her head, for nonmusicians this is simply not possible. However, with the assistance of the website associated with this book, all of the pieces and musical examples in the book can be heard (and downloaded if desired) scrolling in real time with a visual scroll bar as the music is playing, so that no knowledge of musical notation is required. This website opens up the book's musical content and discussion to any listener regardless of musical background, and it allows nonmusicians to have access to a kind of in-depth knowledge usually available only to trained musicians.

In addition to removing the barriers of musical notation for non-musicians, I have tried to remove the barriers of technical vocabulary as well. In general, I have substituted descriptive vocabulary for technical vocabulary whenever possible, and when I have introduced technical terms, I have either immediately explained their meaning in the text itself, or, if they are marked with an asterisk (*), in the glossary at the back of the book. (Musicians can simply skip these explanations.) Though I occasionally mention the names of notes or chords in the text, you do not need to know note or chord names to read this book. Simply think of these names as labels that are marked in the score and can be heard as the scroll bar moves by.

Though this book is obviously meant to be read, it is above all meant to be heard. The words of the text are ultimately nothing but pointers toward musical sounds that I hope you will begin to notice in a new way, and the book is designed to be read and listened to slowly: one piece (one short story) at a time. Some readers might require more than one hearing of each example to fully grasp its content, but by the end of each chapter, with the help of the website, any listener should be able to fulfill Copland's requirement for truly "owning" a piece of music— being able to sing it through in their head from beginning to end. And once you own a Mozart aria or a Chopin mazurka, it can be compared to a Puccini aria or a Dvořák Slavonic dance so that you to begin to get a sense of these composers' different styles as well as a framework for understanding the way musical language changes over time.

Choosing one piece of music to represent a great composer like Mozart or Bach is in some ways an absurd proposition. A single short composition by Chopin or Schubert, like a single painting by Monet or Van Gogh, or a single poem by Walt Whitman or Emily Dickinson, obviously cannot begin to encompass these artists' complete range of achievement or reveal the depth and variety of a lifetime of work; but if looked at in close detail, one great work can serve as a powerful and illuminating point of entry into an artist's creative world. In a quotation that almost defines the purpose of this book, Goethe said, "To know one thing well . . . gives more culture than a half-knowledge of a hundred things." This is a book about knowing one thing well and using that knowledge as a window on a hundred things.

For this book to have the kind of depth I wanted, I had to arbitrarily limit my focus. Music, of course, did not begin with Vivaldi or end with Debussy; however, to do justice to Medieval, Renaissance, and twentieth-century music would require three separate books, so I chose instead to concentrate on short masterpieces from what is generally known as the "common practice period"—the period from Vivaldi to Debussy—written by the period's central, canonical composers. I am by no means claiming that the many composers that I have omitted were not important, did not write great music, or would not be worthy of chapters of their own, but rather that I have chosen depth over breadth, and to gain focus (while avoiding reader exhaustion) have limited the book to the period's eighteen best-known composers.

This book is meant to be a beginning—an entrée into the world of eighteen great composers—not the final word. It makes no pretense of providing a complete view of any single composer but instead offers, paradoxically, a series of in-depth snapshots. Though in many ways this book might seem to be almost diametrically opposed to my first book, it is actually a logical next step. If *All You Have to Do Is Listen* offered a broad approach to listening to music, this book puts that approach into action by applying it to a wide-ranging collection of individual masterpieces spanning almost two hundred years of music. Once you have learned to apply this approach to these pieces, it will not be difficult to move on to other pieces written not only by these eighteen composers but by other composers as well.

One of the things I learned from readers of my first book is that how much you get out of it is directly proportional to how much you put into it. If you take the time to listen carefully to all of the musical examples on the book's website, your ability to richly understand not only the pieces contained in this book but also other music will grow enormously. The Buddhists say if you look closely, you can see the whole world in a single leaf. This is a book about seeing the universal in the particular—the whole in the kernel. All you have to do is listen.

[1]

Antonio Vivaldi
(1678–1741)
"Spring" (Movement 1) from
The Four Seasons

If you don't like this, I'll stop writing music.

—VIVALDI

Fame/Obscurity/Fame

Vivaldi's *Four Seasons* has become one of the most popular pieces of classical music ever written, but its popularity is actually a relatively recent phenomenon. When Vivaldi died in utter poverty in 1741, he was already well on his way to being forgotten—the victim of a fickle public's dramatic shift in musical taste. He was buried in a pauper's grave in a small cemetery in Vienna, and for years no one even knew he had died there, so little was anyone interested in his fate. Though for most of his career as a violinist and a composer he was astonishingly successful, popular, and influential and had composed some five hundred concertos and ninety operas, for two hundred years after his death no one but a few musicologists and historians even knew his name. The twentieth-century Baroque revival brought some renewed interest in his work, but it actually was not until the Italian recording company Cetra put out *The Four Seasons* on 78s in 1950 that Vivaldi was catapulted into the public's imagination.

Given the enormous popularity of these concertos today, the complete confusion surrounding nearly every aspect of their history is surprising. The only thing we know for sure is that *The Four Seasons* was published in 1725 (three years after the first volume of Bach's *Well-Tempered Clavier*) as the first four concertos of a set of twelve entitled "The Contest between Harmony and Invention." However, Vivaldi's dedication to Count Wencelas Morzin apologizes for dedicating pieces the count "already knew," so the music had clearly been written earlier. When, why, and for whom remains a mystery.

The Four Seasons is one of the most thoroughgoing pieces of "program music" ever written, and Vivaldi went to great pains to make the program musically clear. The pieces were published with "descriptive sonnets" prefacing each concerto: each line was given a letter, which was then placed in the score at the appropriate passage, so it would be clear which line of music represented which line of text. Yet we do not know for sure who wrote the sonnets (most scholars think it was Vivaldi) or whether they were written before or after the music.

One of the main reasons Vivaldi did not fade into obscurity was that scholars studying Bach kept coming across his transcriptions of Vivaldi's concertos. Bach's whole approach to the concerto was enormously influenced by arranging six of Vivaldi's concertos for harpsichord, three for organ, and one for four harpsichords and string orchestra. Johann Forkel, Bach's first biographer, said that when Bach transcribed Vivaldi's concertos he wasn't simply trying to learn how to write concertos but that the transcriptions were really a "means to the goal of learning how to think musically." So what did Bach learn from Vivaldi? Let's use what is perhaps the single most famous movement Vivaldi ever wrote—the first movement of "Spring" from *The Four Seasons*—as a window on his musical thinking.

The One vs. the Many

The concerto first appeared as a new form of orchestral composition in the last two decades of the seventeenth century, and it became the single most important type of Baroque orchestral composition after

1700. There were basically two types of Baroque concertos: the concerto grosso, for several soloists and orchestra, and the solo concerto, for a single soloist and orchestra. Both types were fundamentally "about" the deliberate contrast of two different sonorities: a soloist or several soloists and the mass of orchestral sound. The one versus the many. The contrast between the two unequal masses of sound that is at the heart of the concerto is not simply a contrast of volume, but also a contrast of expression. Finding a form that could make effective use of these differences of sound and expression is the essential challenge of the concerto, and Vivaldi's approach ultimately became the dominant model for the Baroque period.

Puccini said that beginnings are everything, and that is one of the keys to Vivaldi's greatness. In the same way that the fundamental character of a theater song is determined by its opening idea (think of "Over the Rainbow" or "I've Got Rhythm"), a Vivaldi concerto movement's fundamental character is determined by its opening orchestral introduction, or *ritornello*.* This opening not only immediately creates the expressive world of the concerto, it also provides the main thematic material for the movement: material that will return (intact or varied) like a refrain to orient the listener. Since the ritornello that opens "Spring" is a perfect example of the style that made Vivaldi famous, let's look closely to see what makes it so great.

EXAMPLE 1

Giuntè la primavera (Spring has arrived)

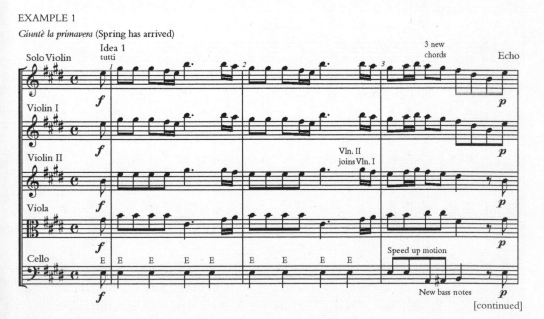

[continued]

EXAMPLE 1 [continued]

"Spring Has Arrived"

Before we even get to the details of the music, the bare numerical facts about this opening are extraordinary. The opening orchestral ritornello lasts for 50 beats. Forty-four of these beats are the same basic E-major chord. In fact, if we include the solo section that follows, 102 of the first 108 beats of the piece are E-major chords! Before Philip Glass and the minimalists arrived on the scene, no piece of music had ever begun with such elementary harmony.

There are actually only two simple ideas in this opening ritornello, but their surface simplicity allows small details to make an enormous impact in ways that can easily be heard and appreciated by any listener. Some of these details are rhythmic. To better appreciate the subtlety of Vivaldi's rhythm, I have written a version of the opening melody that keeps Vivaldi's basic notes but removes his interesting rhythm (example 2A).

If you clap my rhythm of five short notes and one long note twice (sssssl, sssssl), you will immediately get a sense of how lifeless its rhythm is. But notice how the two fast sixteenth notes in Vivaldi's version bring this simple idea to life. Not sssssl, but ssss+*al* (example 2B).

And now a crucial point: from Vivaldi to the twenty-first century, repetition has always been at the heart of comprehensibility. In both music and in life, it is one of the key ways we understand and remember things, and repetition on multiple levels is at the heart of

EXAMPLE 2A

EXAMPLE 2B

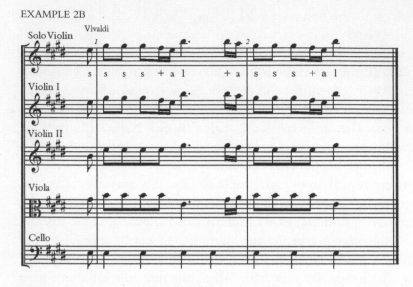

Vivaldi's opening. Every idea in this ritornello is based on inner and self-repetition—repetition within each phrase and of the entire phrase itself—but the repetition is not always as simple as it seems. The opening idea begins with a "leap up" from E to G♯ (example 3A).

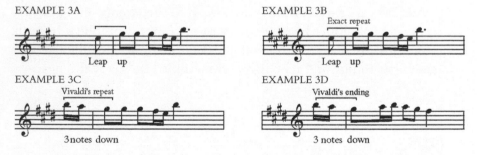

EXAMPLE 3A

EXAMPLE 3B

EXAMPLE 3C

EXAMPLE 3D

An exact repeat would start with the same "leap up" (example 3B). However, Vivaldi replaces it with "three-notes-down": B–A–G♯ (example 3C). And these three notes then become the first three notes of the thought's close (example 3D). Forkel wrote that much of the feeling of inevitability in Bach's music grew out of the fact that "every transition was required to have a connection with the preceding idea and to appear to be a necessary consequence of it," and using part of one idea to generate the music that follows is a technique Bach learned from passages like this one.

Vivaldi uses all the means at his disposal to make the end of this opening phrase beautiful. (See example 1, measures 1 through 3.)

The melody in the first two measures was played by the first violins, with the second violins clearly in an accompanying role. However, in the third measure, the second violins join the first violins at a slightly lower pitch, as if the solo melody has become a duet to close the thought. At the same time, the bass part, which had simply been repeating E's every beat, speeds up and changes notes (and chords) to push to the cadence. To make the key point again, all of these wonderful subtleties—the varied repetition in the melody, the beautiful doubling in the second violins, the acceleration of the bass rhythm, and the change of notes and harmony—are "gettable" on a first hearing. And perhaps most important, the entire opening is a perfect depiction by Vivaldi, the master quick-sketch artist, of the essence of the sonnet's text—"*Giunt'è la primavera*" ("Spring has arrived").

As I mentioned earlier, repetition is one of the keys to Vivaldi's compositional style. We have already looked at the repetition within the opening idea itself. Once we have heard the whole three-measure idea, Vivaldi repeats it in its entirety, but softer, as a classic Baroque echo (example 1, measures 4 through 6). Once again, this kind of echo is an utterly gettable gesture. We hear all the wonderful details of the phrase a second time while enjoying the different sound and feeling of the idea played softer. The surface of the music is everything.

Idea 2

There is only one other idea in this opening ritornello (idea 2 in example 1). This is ultimately the most important theme in the movement, and it operates much like the opening idea in terms of melody, harmony, and repetition. Once again the music makes its points with utter clarity, unmistakable to any listener. Wonderful rhythm leads to and then emphasizes the "money note" in measure 7—the highest note in the introduction. Instead of using four even eighth notes like in example 4A, Vivaldi uses two fast notes to help push to a classic rhythm called a Lombard rhythm or Scotch snap to bring out the highest note (example 4B).

EXAMPLE 4A

Kapilow version

EXAMPLE 4B

Vivaldi   Fast notes   Scotch snap

Vln. I

As in the opening phrase, inner repetition (measure 8) helps the listener remember the catchy idea. Then the Scotch snap in measure 9 generates the final fragment of melody (with a trill to mark the ending of the phrase), while once again, the bass, which had been repeating E's over and over, speeds up and changes notes to drive to the cadence in measure 10. The ritornello ends by echoing the whole idea softer, just as in the opening phrase, firmly implanting the thought in every listener's ear (example 1, measures 10 through 13).

As I mentioned earlier, on the most fundamental level, the Baroque concerto is about the opposition of two different worlds: the world of the soloist or soloists and the world of the ensemble, the *tutti*.* This opposition generates the form of these movements, which basically alternate between solo sections with their own kind of musical speech and group sections that by and large return to music from the opening tutti. Because the contrast between solo and tutti sections is so central to the drama of these concertos, the way each new section begins can provide some of the most striking moments in these pieces, and the arrival and the first solo section of "Spring" are among the most glorious moments in all of Vivaldi.

The Individual versus the Community

A simple way to think of the relationship between the soloist and the orchestra in a concerto is to think in terms of the relationship between individual and community. Though Baroque concertos do, of course, celebrate individual expression and virtuosity, the individual (the soloist) establishes his identity as a participating member of the community (the ensemble) from the concerto's first note. The soloist in "Spring" plays in unison with the ensemble violins throughout the opening ritornello with no compunctions about being an "equal among equals." This is utterly unlike a Classical-period concerto, in which the soloist is clearly "other"—separate from the community—from the very first note, with his absence throughout the opening tutti (except in rare special cases) defining this otherness. In nearly all Baroque concertos, the soloist asserts his special status and assumes a solo role only when the full ensemble drops out to reveal and accompany the already communally active soloist, and the first entrance of the soloist as soloist in "Spring" is one of the most extraordinary textural moments in all of *The Four Seasons*.

EXAMPLE 5

[continued]

EXAMPLE 5 [continued]

"The Birds Greet Her with Glad Song"

So much of Vivaldi's greatness has to do with the surface of things: with small details like trills, ornaments, and decorations. If I were to remove the decorations from the opening of this first solo episode, there would still be the wonderful sense of a new, contrasting sound world emerging as everyone drops out except for the solo violin and one solo violinist from the orchestra.

EXAMPLE 6

However, by removing the decorations from the solo parts, I have removed the essence of the moment in which, as the sonnet tells us, the birds joyfully greet spring with glad song. It is these simple decorations—the *turns** and trills (measures 13 and 14)—that are the key to the new sound world of this first solo section, and it is these simple decorations that turn otherwise ordinary notes into a perfect depiction of birds welcoming spring.

Though the feeling of the music here is anything but mathematical, looking at the numbers in this solo section is even more startling than looking at those in the opening ritornello. There are fifty-eight beats in this section, and all fifty-eight are the same E-major chord! Time feels suspended as all forward motion and harmonic progression stop for this astonishing aviary scene. Though each violinist's fragment of bird music is simple in and of itself, the way all the fragments overlap is magical. The soloist's bird starts singing on a single note decorated with turns (measures 13 and 14), then chirps the same note fourteen times (measures 15 and 16) until a little scale (measures 16 and 17) closes the fragment, with the tiny scale sounding like a bird flowering into song because everything else has been sung on a single note.

EXAMPLE 7

To create the impression of two birds singing from the same family, Vivaldi has one solo violin from the ensemble play the same birdcall in a round, or *canon*,* with the soloist, while adding in a third solo bird as well. Again, in and of itself, this additional fragment of birdsong could not be simpler (see example 5, violin II, measures 14 through 19), but when all three birds are combined, the resulting texture is extraordinary. As this solo section continues, Vivaldi continues to come up with new, imaginative combinations. Each simple birdcall contains some easily gettable musical feature: a hook. One fragment is made up of repeated notes and a trill, done in a round with another solo "bird" from the ensemble.

EXAMPLE 8

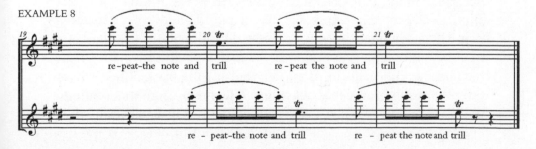

Another snippet is made up of a three-note "whippoorwill" call started by the solo violin (measure 21), then imitated in measure 23 (see example 5, violin I). A long-short, long-short, dotted–rhythm bird gradually speeds up its two-note alternations until they seamlessly turn into a trill.

EXAMPLE 9

Though each of these strands is simple in and of itself, when all of them are combined in the same birdhouse, we get a remarkable texture, suspended within a single E-major harmony for fifty-eight beats, until finally idea 2 from our opening ritornello returns to bring us back to reality and ushers in the full ensemble.

Though this movement contains a good deal of virtuosity for the soloist as it progresses, this opening solo section is a reminder that, above all else, Baroque concertos are about contrasting sonorities. The soloist's music in this section is not particularly difficult to play, and it is no more difficult than the parts for the ensemble. Virtuosity is not the point here. What this section is "about" is the contrast between this wonderful, solo-birdhouse texture and the full–ensemble texture of the opening ritornello. As I mentioned earlier, this contrast is not just a contrast of volume, but also a contrast of expression. Grasping the dramatic possibilities of these kinds of contrasting sound worlds, and placing this drama at the center of the concerto, was Vivaldi's central contribution to the form, and this extraordinary solo section is as perfect an example of Vivaldi's art as you will find anywhere in his concertos.

I mentioned earlier that the opening ritornello of a Vivaldi concerto not only immediately creates the expressive world of the concerto, it also provides the main ensemble material for the movement: material that will return intact, varied, or *transposed** throughout the piece and function like a refrain to orient the listener. Vivaldi rarely brings back his opening ritornello in its entirety but usually brings back one or more of its modular, detachable ideas. These returns give structure to the piece and ensure the familiarity of the original material, while shortening, varying, and transposing the ideas to keep them fresh. The overall form of Vivaldi's concerto movements is as gettable as the ideas they contain. Surprisingly, in "Spring," the opening idea (idea 1) never returns. Though it is one of the best-known melodies in all of Vivaldi's oeuvre, it appears only once. After establishing the tone and atmosphere of the work in a single phrase, it vanishes, leaving only idea 2 to return throughout the movement to represent the ritornello.

"While at Zephyr's Breath the Streams Flow Forth with a Sweet Murmur"

Though there is still scholarly debate over whether these sonnets were written before or after the music, the next solo section seems so perfectly matched to its text that it is hard to imagine the music being created without it. Could there be a more perfect musical depiction of the breath of the wind and the murmuring of the streams than this?

EXAMPLE 10

e i fonti allo spirar de' Zeffiretti con dolce mormorio scorrono intanto.
(while at Zephyr's breath the streams flow forth with a sweet murmur.)

[continued]

EXAMPLE 10 [continued]

[continued]

EXAMPLE 10 [continued]

Vivaldi's astonishing ability to instantly evoke a poetic image runs throughout the movement. The sudden switch to the whole orchestra playing incredibly fast notes in unison followed by scales shooting upward in the violins thrillingly depicts the thunder and lightning of the sonnet text. Once again the idea is utterly clear and dramatically effective.

EXAMPLE 11

Vengon coprendo l'aer di nero ammanto e lampi e tuoni ad annunziarla eletti;
(Her chosen heralds, thunder and lightning, come to envelop the air in a black cloak;)

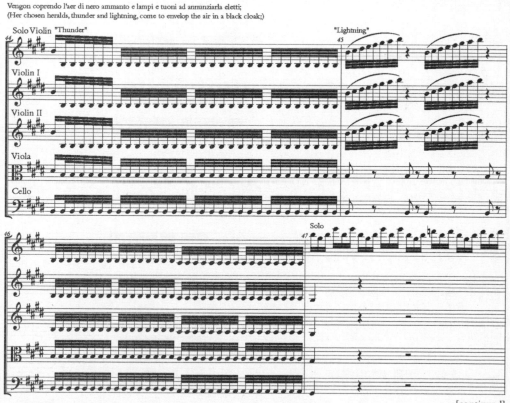

[continued]

EXAMPLE 11 [continued]

[continued]

EXAMPLE 11 [continued]

"Her Chosen Heralds, Thunder and Lightning, Come to Envelop the Air in a Black Cloak"

The heightened drama of the spring storm generates the virtuosity of the solo section that follows. If the contrast between two unequal masses of sound is what concertos are all about, then this passage is a perfect example. The entire ensemble plays powerfully in unison in contrast with the solo violin, while the soloist's furious virtuosity allows him to hold his own. One of the keys to Vivaldi, for which he is often criticized, is his use (or overuse) of sequences—passages in which a short musical idea is repeated several times, each time starting on a different note. Like the straightforward repetition of a musical idea, or an echo, repeating an idea in a sequence is an extremely effective way of creating dramatic tension. The sonnet's storm generates a fast, virtuosic solo violin idea (example 11, measure 47) alternating with the thunder music in the orchestra (measure 48). The whole combination is sequenced higher in measures 48 and 49, and then sequenced higher again as the storm grows more intense. The sequence varies its shape and changes direction as the storm picks up speed, and the thunder entries come faster and faster until the section ends with the first minor-key cadence of the piece (measure 55).

In terms of the movement's overall form, each section that depicts a scene from the sonnet is bracketed by a return of idea 2 from the opening ritornello, and these returns give structure and coherence to the piece. Idea 2 always comes back shortened without echo. The first two times it returns in a major key, but by the third return, the storm and lightning have shifted the emotional landscape, and in a powerful moment of transformation, idea 2 comes back for the first time in a minor key.

EXAMPLE 12

indi tacendo questi gl'augelletti tornan di nuovo al lor canoro incanto:
(once they have fallen silent, the little birds return anew to their melodious incantation:)

[continued]

EXAMPLE 12 [continued]

Return of full ensemble

"Once They [Thunder and Lightning] Have Fallen Silent, the Little Birds Return Anew to Their Melodious Incantation"

Though the sonnets that are the basis for these concertos are by no means great poetry, they add a programmatic meaning and a specificity to Vivaldi's musical ideas that transform their sense and significance. On a purely musical level, the material of the next section could not be more elementary. Over a held note in the cello and bass, the soloist repeats a single note and then rises up a simple *chromatic scale** (example 12, measures 59 and 60). A soloist from the ensemble imitates (measures 61 and 62). A third soloist enters, they all exchange a simple two-note figure, and the combination speeds up. However, when we listen to this passage with the sonnet's text in mind, it becomes a stunning musical painting of one, then two, then three birds hesitantly stepping out of hiding to see if the spring storm has ended. They then begin to warble as a trio—first tentatively and then with growing energy—until their confidence finally brings in the whole flock: the entire string ensemble. The combination of the sonnet and the music is pure magic, and program music does not get more captivating than this.

The variety of sound worlds Vivaldi is able to create out of his basic Baroque string ensemble is amazing, and the orchestral texture changes one more time as we suddenly seem to be listening to an intimate solo violin sonata with continuo accompaniment (cello, bass, and harpsichord). This thin two-part texture (example 13, measures 70 through 75) makes the return of the tutti (measure 76) sound rich and full in comparison, and the concerto finishes with a perfect musical bookend. Idea 2 returns in its original version with echo, and Vivaldi ends where he began. The birds, the key of E major, and the music of the opening ritornello have all returned, and all is well in Vivaldi's universe. Spring has arrived.

EXAMPLE 13

In Sync with the Zeitgeist

An artist does not ultimately get to choose his voice. Some composers, like Vivaldi, were lucky enough to have a voice that was in sync with the zeitgeist—the spirit of the times—for a large portion of their careers, while others, like Bach, were not. Vivaldi used to boast that he could write a concerto faster than a copyist could copy it. Contemporaries talked about his fantastic energy; too much mercury, they said. Vivaldi's musical personality combined a performer's audience-pleasing virtuosity with a theater composer's dramatic flair. He also had the good fortune of having an ear that was fascinated by music with the kind of alive, dramatic, sensuous surface that was immediately gettable by his audience. Vivaldi responded to music like his audience did. The virtuosity, drama, rhythm, clarity of form, and contrasts of sound that entranced Vivaldi entranced his audiences as well and, after a long period of obscurity, continue to entrance audiences today.

There is no doubt that Bach admired and was influenced by the directness, simplicity, drama, and clarity of Vivaldi's music, but ultimately Bach could no more write like Vivaldi than Faulkner could write like Hemingway. Every artist ultimately offers an inherently limited view of the world as seen from his own, unique perspective. The greatest artists accept these limitations and embrace both what they are and what they are not, and we must do the same as listeners. The brilliant writer on mythology Joseph Campbell wrote, "The privilege of a lifetime is being who you are." This is a book about eighteen composers who became who they were. Some, like Vivaldi, Puccini, Verdi, and Dvořák, were fortunate enough to be in sync with the zeitgeist for significant portions of their careers and attained enormous popularity. Others, like Bach and Schumann, were almost completely unheralded during their lifetimes and attained "canonical" status only after their deaths. All of the common practice period's great composers, from Vivaldi to Debussy, had a unique kind of greatness to offer that is still there today, waiting to be discovered, measure by measure, and season by season.

[2]

Johann Sebastian Bach
(1685–1750)
Invention No. 1 from
The Two-part Inventions

———

Bach taught me the art of creating the whole from a single kernel.

—ARNOLD SCHOENBERG

Had he been alive in 1985, Bach would surely have been astonished to see the celebrations surrounding his three-hundredth birthday. During his lifetime, he was primarily known as an organ virtuoso and a composer of complex contrapuntal works. There were many other composers far more famous than he was, and by the end of his life, his style of contrapuntal music was completely out of fashion. None of his contemporaries would have dreamed that more than 250 years after his death, he would be considered one of the greatest composers of all time. Unlike Beethoven, who regarded himself as an artistic genius whose music would live on forever, Bach regarded himself as a dedicated craftsman doing a job in the service of his patron and his listeners.

As he grew older, concerned that the craft he had devoted his life to was vanishing, Bach embarked on a remarkable series of works designed to summarize and codify the possibilities of this dying style.

Works like *A Musical Offering, The Art of Fugue, The Goldberg Variations, The Well-Tempered Clavier*, and the Mass in B Minor are encyclopedic demonstrations of the range of Bach's achievement in instrumental and sacred music; however, he was interested in passing on his knowledge not only to the musical world at large but also to his own children, and in 1723 he completed a music instruction book for his eldest son, Wilhelm Friedemann Bach, called the *Klavierbüchlein* (Little Clavier Book). The work included fifteen two- and three-part inventions (*Inventiones* and *Sinfoniae*), and though it was not published during Bach's lifetime, it circulated widely in manuscript copies before its first publication in 1801. Today we tend to think of composition and instrumental performance as two separate disciplines, but it is clear that for Bach they were intimately connected. In his foreword to the 1723 autograph of the *Klavierbüchlein*, he states clearly that the collection's purpose is not only to be "a proper introduction, whereby lovers of the clavier . . . are shown a clear way of learning to play cleanly in two voices," but also an introduction on "how to compose good inventions and develop them well . . . and [how] to acquire a taste for the elements of composition."

At first glance the term "invention" seems to be an odd title for a piece of music, and its use as a musical title is almost exclusively confined to Bach. The word actually comes from the field of rhetoric and refers to the Roman orator Cicero's five stages in creating an oration: invention (*inventio*), arrangement (*dispositio*), style (*elocutio*), memory (*memoria*), and delivery (*pronuntiatio*). According to Cicero, "One must first hit upon what to say; then manage and marshal his discoveries, not merely in orderly fashion, but with a discriminating eye for the exact weight, as it were, of each argument; next go on to array them in the adornments of style; after that keep them guarded in his memory; and in the end deliver them with effect and charm." In essence, this is exactly what the Two-part Inventions were designed to teach—the art of discovering an excellent musical idea that could be used as a compositional theme (an invention) and the means of developing that idea into a complete composition. Since these two-part inventions were originally designed to be a succinct introduction to the basic elements of Bach's compositional craft, they can serve a similar purpose in this chapter as we use the well-known Two-part Invention in C Major as a means of seeing how Bach turns rhetoric into music.

The Art of Invention: Becoming versus Being

We have already discussed Vivaldi's remarkable ability to create striking musical ideas that instantly capture the listener's attention, but Vivaldi's "inventions" operate in a completely different way from Bach's. To slightly oversimplify, though Vivaldi's musical ideas are certainly developed and transformed over the course of a movement (we saw the powerful effect of bringing back the main ritornello idea of "Spring" shifted into a minor key), they are fundamentally designed to make their impression as first heard. Vivaldi might echo, repeat, transpose, or shift an idea from a major key to a minor key, but he rarely transforms its core identity. Vivaldi's ideas exist, so to speak, in the present tense.

Bach, however, is primarily interested in the future tense. In becoming, not in being. For him, what is most important is not what a musical idea is, but what it can develop into. Arnold Schoenberg said that Bach taught him "the art of creating the whole from a single kernel," and the ability to create a dazzlingly rich composition out of a single musical idea is in many respects the essence of Bach's art. Quite often the "kernel" or "invention" that is at the heart of a work by Bach is so brief and unmemorable that it seems almost inconceivable that such a short, undistinguished idea could possibly be the basis for an entire composition. Many of his most powerful fugues work with deliberately plain subjects chosen precisely for their "non-flashiness"—for their ability to combine with other music in continually changing contexts as the piece progresses. They are pure potentiality. Like the kernels of the Two-part Inventions, their meaning becomes clear only over time, when the piece has finished and we look back and marvel at how "this" (the fugue, or invention—the whole) could have come from "that" (the subject—the kernel).

Invention I

One of the main challenges for young performers in learning to play Bach's Two-part Inventions is the complete independence of the two hands. Unlike so much of the music written for intermediate-level pianists, which puts nearly all of the difficult material in the right hand accompanied by an elementary left hand, the Two-part Inventions have material of equal importance and equal difficulty in both hands. This independence of the hands is a challenge not only for the performer but also for the listener, who must hear both parts separately to truly appreciate Bach's musical thought.

The "invention," or main idea, that is at the heart of the C-Major Two-part Invention is a classic example of a Bach idea whose meaning perpetually evolves as the piece progresses. Questions and possibilities begin with the very first measure of the piece as we try to discover what the topic, or main theme, of the composition actually is. Since the entire piece will grow out of this one idea, let's look closely at how it is made.

EXAMPLE 1

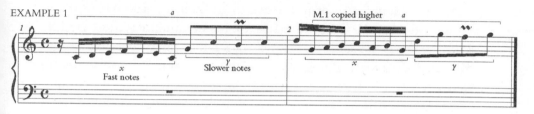

Like so many Bach ideas, this one gains energy by beginning off the beat, and its syncopated start makes the idea immediately recognizable whenever it recurs. If you simply play the right hand alone in the first two measures, the makeup of the theme seems clear. The idea of measure 1—call it "a"—is made up of two tiny motives—one in fast notes (x) and one in slower notes (y). When the right hand repeats the whole idea higher in measure 2, it seems to confirm our understanding of the main theme. Bach's "invention" is one measure long, made up of two short motives. However, when we examine the left hand of these two measures, our understanding begins to change.

EXAMPLE 2

Bach begins to work with and develop motives from the main theme in the very first measure of the piece. The left hand enters as if to copy the entire one-measure idea of the right hand, but instead copies only the first part—the fast notes, not the slow notes. Eliminating part of a theme tells us what is essential and what is inessential, and already in the first measure of the piece, Bach is showing us that the theme's essential core is its fast notes. The right hand plays the whole idea (a), while the left hand extracts its essence (x).

Upside Down

One of the extraordinary things about this piece and so many other works by Bach is the pace of the musical thought: the speed at which ideas are developed. Only seconds into the piece (example 3, measure 3), Bach suddenly transforms the opening idea in a startling way as the right hand takes the fast notes of the theme (x) and turns them upside down (xi). (*Upside down*, or *inverted*, means that each ascending interval becomes a descending interval and vice versa. In this case, a four-note scale going up becomes a four-note scale going down, and two downward leaps become two ascending leaps.) As if this isn't enough development for one measure, at the same time, the left hand takes the opening four-note scale and stretches each note rhythmically (example 4, x+).

Stravinsky said that all composition ultimately comes down to a balance between unity and variety. Too much unity (too much repetition) leads to boredom, while too much variety (too much contrast) leads to chaos. This third measure is a perfect example of Bach's sublime balance of unity and variety. The new musical combination sounds remarkably different from the original version—the essence of "variety" in Stravinsky's terms—however, every note is derived from the opening idea.

What happens from here till the end of the phrase brilliantly demonstrates what Bach's consummate craft is all about. Having turned the opening idea upside down (xi), the right hand immediately repeats this new, upside-down version three more times, each time lower, so that it will cement itself in the listener's ear (measures 3 through 5).

EXAMPLE 3

The left hand repeats its accompanying idea lower as well (x+), and Bach could easily have repeated it four times as in the right hand.

EXAMPLE 4

However, instead of repeating the figure a fourth time (unity/variety), Bach continues the four-note scale two notes higher, turning it into a powerful six-note scale (x6) that drives the music forward.

EXAMPLE 5

Here is the passage with both hands:

EXAMPLE 6

The Push toward Home

After a repeat of measure 1 a step higher, the compositional fireworks begin, and they create an irresistible push to the cadence. Like so much Baroque music, the C-Major Invention establishes a basic rhythm and texture at the opening that continues without interruption to the end. This seamless, rhythmic flow gives the piece an infectious, "foot-tapping" energy and momentum; however, it places great structural emphasis on the three cadences in the piece (measure 7, measure 15, and the final measure), as they are the invention's only significant points of rest and arrival. To follow everything that is going on in this push to the piece's first cadence, let's look first at the right hand and then at the left hand.

EXAMPLE 7

Bach states his upside-down idea one more time in the right hand (xi in measure 5), and then takes just its ending—its last four notes (call it xi4)—and uses that ending to rise higher and higher. This kind of breaking down of a musical idea into smaller and smaller fragments in order to drive to the cadence is classic Bach technique (like tightening a screw dramatically), as is the way he uses completely new music not heard before in the piece in order to help clearly articulate this key moment of arrival.

EXAMPLE 8

At the same time all of this compositional activity is happening in the right hand, the left hand is helping to drive to the cadence as well. Nothing is wasted in Bach, not even the most seemingly insignificant ideas, and he now begins to work not just with his main theme but with his own earlier developments of that theme. In the second half of measure 5, the left hand takes what had initially seemed to be a momentary decoration—the scale with the extra two notes in measure 4 (x6)—and uses it again: this time to accompany the new developments in the right hand. And finally, like the right hand, the left hand brings in a completely new rhythm and melodic figure to clarify and underline the cadence. The entire phrase has pushed toward this arrival, and Bach makes sure that we will not miss this key dramatic moment.

"The Whole from the Kernel"

So much of Bach's compositional style is contained in this one brilliant phrase. The amount of imaginative activity and the sheer concentration of musical thought is staggering. The opening invention has already been transposed, shortened to its first fragment, turned upside down, stretched rhythmically, and reduced to its upside-down ending in the first twenty seconds of the piece! Every moment counts in Bach. There is absolutely no "filler." Like each sentence in a masterful oration by Cicero, each measure moves the argument forward. Every note in both hands is derived from the main theme—the whole has been created from a single kernel—and the only music not specifically derived from that kernel has intentionally been used to underline the cadence that ends the section.

What is even more remarkable is that every one of the remaining measures of the piece is derived from the opening idea as well! For those interested in following this out in bar-by-bar detail, I have included a complete analysis of the rest of the piece in example 11, but what I want to focus on here is not so much the measure-by-measure minutiae but several broader issues that relate not only to this piece but to Bach's style as a whole. One thing that is important to understand is that the C–Major Invention and pieces like it are much more than a simple stringing together of successive developments of a main theme. Once Bach has developed a germ idea into an opening phrase, various groups of measures within that phrase, or even the entire phrase as a whole, can become a new topic to work with as the piece progresses. For example, the second section of the invention instantly begins to develop not just the opening one-measure idea, but also the opening two measures of the piece as a unit.

EXAMPLE 9

We have already seen Bach turn an individual musical idea upside down, but he now turns an entire musical combination upside down. If you look at example 9, you can see that the hands have exchanged parts. The right hand of measures 1 and 2 has become the left hand of measures 7 and 8, while the left hand of measures 1 and 2 has become the right hand of measures 7 and 8 (both hands are transposed a fifth). What was on top is now on bottom, and what was on bottom is now on top. This kind of flipping of parts (technically called *invertible counterpoint**) changes the entire sound of the combination, and Bach uses this device in nearly all of his contrapuntal pieces. However, it is important to understand that in turning this opening combination upside down, Bach is also beginning to expand the main idea itself by working now with a two-measure unit, not just a single-measure idea.

Two measures later, Bach expands the thought even further and

EXAMPLE 10

begins to work with a four-measure unit. If you compare the right hand of measures 3 through 7 in example 10 with the left hand of measures 11 through 15, you will see that the parts have not only been flipped (and transposed), but have also shifted from major to minor. As we saw with Vivaldi, shifting a theme from a major key to a minor key creates a potent dramatic effect, and in this invention, the shift to a minor key, while both parts are simultaneously being flipped and transposed, is a major compositional event. (If you look at example 11, you will see that the right-hand part is flipped and varied as well.)

We have already seen Bach expand his compositional thought from a one-measure idea to a two-measure and finally a four-measure idea; however, if you look in example 11 at the second section as a whole (measures 7 through 14), you can see that, with a pause for two new measures in measures 9 and 10, the entire second section is actually the opening six-measure phrase flipped upside down! The entire first phrase has now become the compositional unit. This kind of approach to structure can be found throughout Bach's works. Like the ripples that spread out when you throw a pebble into a lake, the musical thought is continually expanding as the piece moves forward. The meaning of the opening theme is evolving as the work progresses, and its structure is being generated before our very eyes.

The Final Phrase

Having reached the point furthest from "home" harmonically in the piece—A minor—the final phrase (measure 15 through the end) must find its way back home to C major, and if you look at example 11 you will see that once again it does so not simply by developing material from the main theme, but by developing earlier blocks of material. The first four measures of the phrase (measures 15 through 18) vary two measures from section II (measures 9 and 10), and in a classic balance of unity and variety that almost defines Bach's art, the final measures of all three sections of the piece work with the same basic material (xi and x+), but each phrase develops the material in a completely different way. Every measure in the piece grows out of the opening "invention," yet no two measures are the same. Cicero's rhetoric has been turned into music in a stunning display of "the art of creating the whole from a single kernel."

EXAMPLE 11

Constraint and Freedom

In *Poetics of Music in the Form of Six Lessons*, Stravinsky wrote,

> The more art is controlled, limited, worked over, the more it is free. My freedom thus consists in my moving about within the narrow frame that I have assigned myself for each one of my undertakings. I shall go even farther: my freedom will be so much the greater and more meaningful the more narrowly I limit my field of action and the more I surround myself with obstacles. The more constraints one imposes the more one frees oneself of the chains that shackle the spirit.

Stravinsky's provocative idea that constraint in art produces freedom is at the heart of Bach's greatness. All of Bach's contrapuntal works, like the Two-part Inventions and the fugues from *The Well-Tempered Clavier* and *The Art of Fugue*, are defined by freedom within extraordinary constraints. Their single-minded focus on one idea forces Bach to find the whole hidden in the kernel. Yet even Bach's noncontrapuntal works tend to work within similar constraints. One of the most important theoretical ideas running throughout the seventeenth and eighteenth centuries was the so-called "doctrine of the affections." The theory of the "affections" held that the basic germ of a composition, its fundamental idea, was a tangible embodiment of a particular affect: an emotional state of being. Once the fundamental idea of a movement established an affect, the rest of the movement would be an elaboration or exploration of that affect: an exploration of a single emotional state and a single idea.

One of the principal differences between the Baroque and Classical styles, as we will see when we get to the chapters on Haydn, Mozart, and Beethoven, is a fundamentally different concept of musical drama. Once a movement of Bach establishes its basic rhythm and texture, it normally continues uninterrupted until the final cadence, and this homogeneity of texture and rhythm is matched by a constant level of dramatic tension that rarely rises significantly above the level set at the opening of the movement. To slightly oversimplify, a Classical-period sonata is about dramatic contrast and dramatic action, whereas a Bach fugue or invention is essentially rhetorical. It is more like an essay than a novel, more like a compelling argument than a dramatic narrative. As pianist/scholar Charles Rosen puts it poetically, "A Baroque piece is a dramatic image, a single dramatized emotion, not a dramatic scenario." Bach examines a single theme in order to understand its rhetorical possibilities, not its potential for dramatic narrative.

An obituary of Bach published in 1754 stated that he "needed only to hear a theme to be aware—it seemed instantaneously—of almost every intricacy an artist could produce in treating it." In the end, what a great work like the C-Major Two-part Invention offers is the enormous satisfaction of hearing a single idea, a single affect, explored completely. In a strange way, Bach's music is deeply democratic. It does not matter whether the musical idea at the heart of one of his pieces is exotic and distinctive, or plain and undistinguished. Every musical idea seems to have equally rich possibilities, and Bach explores them all. At the end of each movement we are left with the profound sense of having explored the depths of one thing. His music ultimately offers a satisfaction similar to that of a life well lived. A life that has utilized its full potential and realized all of its possibilities. A life dedicated to realizing the whole hidden in each kernel.

[3]

George Frideric Handel
(1685–1759)
"Hallelujah Chorus" from *Messiah*

———————

Handel is so great and so simple that no one but a professional musician is unable to understand him.

—SAMUEL BUTLER

"Forever and Ever"

At the end of chapter 1, I said that certain composers, like Vivaldi, were lucky enough to have a voice that was in sync with the zeitgeist, while others, like Bach, were not. Some composers were famous during their lifetimes and then disappeared forever, while others lived in relative obscurity, only to be resurrected years later. Handel, however, was world-renowned during his lifetime, and his fame has never declined. He was the dominant figure of his era in English music and was buried with full public honors in Westminster Abbey, but both his career and his music were thoroughly international. Born and trained in Germany, he spent significant, formative time in Italy laying the foundation for his operatic career before moving to England, where he spent nearly all of his mature artistic years and became a British citizen in 1726.

Today Handel is known to the general public primarily as a composer of oratorios and one instrumental piece, *Water Music*, but for thirty-five years his principal occupation was composing, conducting, and producing Italian opera. By 1740, however, his reputation in the field had waned, his opera company had been downsized out of existence, and at age fifty-five he was forced to reinvent himself with a new form of dramatic music—oratorio in the English language, designed to be performed in the theater during Lent. His first two oratorios, *Saul* and *Israel in Egypt*, met with mixed receptions, and Handel was unsure if the form was even viable. When he received an invitation from the Lord Lieutenant of Ireland to write a new oratorio, it was the first time in thirty years that he had been asked to compose a work for performance outside of London.

Though we tend to think of that oratorio, *Messiah*, as the quintessential Handel oratorio, it was actually unique in many ways for Handel. As conductor/musicologist Christopher Hogwood points out,

> It is the only truly "sacred" oratorio he ever wrote, it was the only one performed during his lifetime in a consecrated building, and yet it was intended, in his librettist's words, as "a fine entertainment" . . . Although quintessentially the work of a theatre composer, it contains no drama in the theatrical sense; there are no warring factions (no Israelites versus Philistines), no named protagonist . . . The drama is revealed obliquely, by inference and report, almost never by narrative.

Messiah is as unoperatic as any oratorio Handel would ever write. The original idea of oratorio was that it should be a kind of sacred opera used for religious instruction, and Handel ordinarily took every opportunity to capitalize on the texts' dramatic situations. But *Messiah* is different. The text, compiled by the literary scholar Charles Jennens, is a skillfully arranged collection of Old and New Testament quotations that progress from Prophecy through Nativity, Crucifixion, Resurrection, and Ascension to the Promise of Redemption. However, Handel's treatment of these quotations is more reflective commentary than drama, and the chorus, which is almost nonexistent in Baroque opera, lies at the center of the work. *Messiah* is a piece of gigantic scope containing an enormous variety of music. Much of the most wonderful music is for solo voices; however, the heart of the piece is choral, and since it is the heart of the piece and Handel's genius that I want to discuss in this chapter, let's look closely at the most famous piece of music Handel ever wrote: the chorus that concludes part two of *Messiah*—the "Hallelujah Chorus."

Because this chorus is so well known, it is almost possible to forget how amazing it is. The ecstatic text is drawn from Revelation and depicts the miraculous moment when the world finally and forever becomes heavenly: the moment when "the Kingdom of this world" becomes "the Kingdom of our Lord, forever and ever." Let's see if we can strip away the movement's iconic status and get at what makes it so great.

"Sticky" Ideas

In his book *The Tipping Point*, Malcolm Gladwell talks about how advertisers are always searching for "sticky" ideas—ideas or logos that will quickly "stick" in the public's mind and be easily remembered. For example, "Winston tastes good like a cigarette should," in which both the rhyme (good/should) and the incorrect grammar ("like," not "as") help make the phrase memorable. Handel's greatness begins with his uncanny ability to create sticky ideas that are not only musically memorable but also somehow manage to convey the essence of a text's meaning in just a few notes. Often the tiniest difference can turn an ordinary idea into an unforgettable one. If you take the four famous first notes of the "Hallelujah Chorus" and alter their rhythm so that every note lasts one beat, it would sound like this:

EXAMPLE 1

"Hallelujah," in this square, wooden version is utterly nonecstatic. If we double the speed of "lu-jah," the idea becomes slightly more interesting but is still relatively ordinary.

EXAMPLE 2

What makes it thrilling is Handel's lengthening of the first note. The sustained "Ha" grows in energy until it spills over into the excited, quicker-by-contrast "le-lu-jah" (with a fantastic syncopated "le"), and the four-note combination is classic Handel: musically memorable and a perfect depiction of the word's meaning.

EXAMPLE 3

Handel's musical thought, like Bach's, moves at an incredibly fast pace. This opening idea gets repeated only once before it is immediately varied.

Two wonderfully fast notes, faster than any notes in the piece so far ("Hal-le," upbeat to measure 6), start the new idea with a jolt, and this idea also repeats only once to let us know that it's an idea. (Notice how Handel makes sure we don't miss these wonderfully "sticky" fast notes, as he echoes them in the strings every time they are sung by the chorus.) When the third and final idea surprises us by *not* repeating itself to complete the opening thought (making an irregular-sounding

EXAMPLE 4

[continued]

EXAMPLE 4 [continued]

four-measure phrase after the three-measure orchestral introduction), we notice something wonderful retrospectively about this vocal phrase, though its true significance will not become clear till the last measure of the piece. Each of the three versions of "Hallelujah" has accented a different syllable. The first version accents "ha": "*HAl*-le-lu-jah." The second version accents "lu": "Hal-le-*LU*-jah," and the third version accents "le": "Hal-*LE*-lu-jah." Three different ways to hear a single word. Three different ways to rejoice.

As I mentioned in our discussion of Vivaldi, repetition in music and in life is one of the key ways we understand and remember things, and we find the same kinds of repetition in Handel's music that we found in Vivaldi's. "Spring," you may remember, began with a three-part idea based on inner repetition, followed by an echo of the entire phrase. Repeating a whole block of music tells the listener that the entire block, not just a single segment, is the idea. Handel, as we have just seen, also begins with a three-part idea based on inner repetition, followed by a repeat of the entire phrase to let the listener know that the whole combination—all three ideas together—is "the idea." But instead of repeating the idea note-for-note like Vivaldi, Handel repeats the idea transposed, that is, starting on a different note.

EXAMPLE 5

"For the Lord God Omnipotent Reigneth"

As I mentioned a moment ago, a sticky idea for Handel is one that is
not just musically memorable but one that also somehow manages
to convey the essence of a text's meaning in just a few notes, and
Handel's ability to continually come up with the perfect musical
idea to bring a text to life is at the heart of his greatness. To convey
the power of the pronouncement "For the Lord God omnipotent
reigneth," the thick, opening orchestral/choral texture ceases, and
suddenly both the orchestra and the chorus speak in unison, as if
they have become a single, unified congregation, connected by one
faith, singing the same notes together, underlining and dramatizing
the musical thought (example 6).

After the chorus interjects ecstatic "hallelujahs" (with added trumpets and timpani) to show the feeling evoked by this pronouncement,
the chorus repeats the idea, again in unison, but transposed lower
(measures 17 through 19), giving the words an even more solemn feel
in this lower vocal range. Handel was extraordinarily sensitive to the
dramatic possibilities of different registers both in the human voice
and in instruments. He frequently uses extreme high registers as well

EXAMPLE 6

[continued]

EXAMPLE 6 [continued]

as extreme low registers to convey particular emotional states, and as we shall see, much of the drama of the "Hallelujah Chorus" is deeply connected to range and register both vocally and instrumentally.

One of the wonderful things about presenting an idea in unison is that it allows a composer the chance to replay the idea later with accompanying music that can give it a dramatically different meaning. After the idea is introduced twice in unison, it returns ecstatically, an octave higher in the sopranos, while the rest of the chorus interjects glorious "hallelujahs" underneath (example 7).

In this passage, Handel stunningly combines two ideas that had previously been kept separate—"unison awe" and "ecstatic hallelujahs." This is much more than a mere technical feat: the simple case of a musical idea in unison returning later with an accompaniment. This new combination represents a completely different emotional attitude toward the idea of the Lord God reigning omnipotent. Handel uses Bach's contrapuntal technique for his own theatrical purposes to create emotional drama within music of a single affect. Even Bach's familiar procedure of flipping musical combinations upside down is put to striking effect here, as Handel flips this new combination upside down and puts the "unison pronouncement" in the men's voices underneath the "interjecting" hallelujahs in the women's voices (example 8).

EXAMPLE 7

EXAMPLE 8

[continued]

EXAMPLE 8 [continued]

Orchestration

Before we look at two of the greatest moments in the piece, I need to quickly point out something about the orchestration of *Messiah*. In spite of the influence of the period-instrument movement, which has led to many intimate, small-chorus performances of *Messiah*, for many people *Messiah* still conjures up the image of an enormous chorus of Mormon Tabernacle proportions performing in a cavernous cathedral with a huge orchestra dominated by majestic trumpets and timpani. If you study the score, however, one of the most striking things about the piece is the economy of its orchestration. In the original version that Handel wrote for Dublin, forty-nine of the fifty-three movements are scored for nothing but a string section and keyboard continuo accompaniment. A single trumpet accompanies the aria "The Trumpet Shall Sound," offstage trumpets appear in "Glory to God," and trumpets and timpani appear, to the dismay of budget-conscious presenters everywhere, in only two movements: the "Hallelujah Chorus" and the final chorus that ends the work. Consequently, in a full performance of *Messiah*, the first onstage appearance of trumpets and timpani in the "Hallelujah Chorus," after nearly an hour of strings and keyboard, is electrifying.

The trumpets and timpani first enter in measure 14 and immediately add power and drama to the scene, as they reinforce and accompany the "interjecting" hallelujahs (measures 14 through 33). However, it is their impact on the next passage that is truly unforgettable. As I mentioned earlier, the text for this key passage depicts the miraculous moment when the world finally and forever becomes heavenly. The moment when "the kingdom of this world" becomes "the kingdom of our Lord and of his Christ forever and ever."

"The Kingdom of This World"

Great composers do not set words to music; they set the emotions behind the words. In and of themselves, the words that describe this moment, "The kingdom of this world is become the kingdom of our Lord," seem far too brief to support the extraordinary musical drama that Handel creates; however, as we have already seen with Vivaldi, a great composer can bring a text to life in an instant. What makes this moment so unique is that Handel paints the actual moment of transformation itself. The preceding section ends with trumpet and timpani flourishes in the rhythm of "hallelujah" still ringing in our ears. The words that begin the new section are "The kingdom of this world," but what Handel really sets to music is the radiant calm of "the kingdom of this world" as seen from on high in Heaven. The trumpets and timpani drop out, the complex contrapuntal writing ceases, and the chorus sings in pure chordal fashion, accompanied only by the string section (example 9).

EXAMPLE 9

Everything combines to make the serenity of this moment magical. The choralelike voice parts with their simple stepwise melody are all in wonderfully calm, low registers. In addition, the dramatic instrumental contrast between the ringing trumpets and timpani that ended the preceding section and the string-accompanied chorus is deepened by two brief beats in which the strings play by themselves (measures 35 and 36). When this extraordinary phrase, "The kingdom of this world is become," briefly pauses on an utterly peaceful cadence with all four choral voice parts in their most relaxed registers (measure 37), Handel has somehow taken us from the ecstatic, energetic, contrapuntal world of the opening to a moment of almost surreal calm in only four measures.

"The Kingdom of Our Lord"

Having reached this brief moment of exquisite stillness, we suddenly witness the transformation of "the kingdom of this world" into "the kingdom of our Lord" right before our eyes in one extraordinary beat of music (measure 37). Handel violates all of the textbook rules of "proper" *voice leading** as the four voice parts simultaneously leap upward with the two outer voices, the bass and soprano, leaping up an *octave** and a *tenth** respectively! At the same moment, all of the string parts leap upward as well, as the trumpets (and timpani) enter gloriously in their upper registers. In a thrilling orchestral moment, the first trumpet soars triumphantly above the entire chorus to play the main melody—the serene, soprano notes of "The kingdom of this world" now thrillingly transposed an octave higher—as if it were "the seventh trumpet heralding the reign of Christ" in the book of Revelation.

"King of Kings and Lord of Lords"

This moment exemplifies what Handel brought to the world of the oratorio, as he uses the full dramatic arsenal of a High Baroque opera composer to bring this imagined biblical event vividly to life. But as wonderful as this moment is, it is actually the section that follows that is the most famous and thrilling part of the piece: Handel's setting of what would seem to be a completely undramatic text, "king of kings and lord of lords." At first glance, these words seem to be nothing more than a descriptive renaming or relabeling of God. Who is he? "King of kings, and lord of lords." The basic musical idea of the passage could not be simpler: a single note repeated over and over again.

EXAMPLE 10

However, the drama that Handel creates out of this elementary musical idea and simple text is astonishing. The phrase begins with the musical equivalent of a "split-screen" effect in the chorus. The women, in one emotional plane, solemnly pronounce "king of kings, and lord of lords" on a single note in an even, sustained rhythm, while the men convey the community's excited reaction to the prospect of God's eternal reign through their ecstatic interjections: "forever and ever, hallelujah, hallelujah!"

EXAMPLE 11

[continued]

EXAMPLE 11 [continued]

[continued]

EXAMPLE 11 [continued]

Handel then starts to transpose the whole passage higher, and the higher, more intense vocal range increases the urgency of the phrase. In the hands of a great composer, changing one note can make an enormous difference. If Handel had copied "king of kings and lord of lords" on a single note as he did the first time, it would have gone like this:

EXAMPLE 12

However, this time "And Lord of Lords" rises a step higher on "Lord."

EXAMPLE 13

The excitement becomes almost unbearable as Handel keeps rising higher and higher, with each melody note, "forever," and "hallelujah" more ecstatic than the previous one. All the while, the first trumpet is doubling the choral melody, adding brilliance to the rising line until finally, at the top of the soprano's vocal range, the phrase climaxes radiantly on a G and returns the music to the home key. Now everything is resolved. "King of Kings" comes back lower.

EXAMPLE 14

[continued]

EXAMPLE 14 [continued]

And when it returns one final time at the end of the piece, it runs right into "hallelujah," all on a single note in the soprano's melody. All on a D. We have reached heaven, where all themes combine—"king of kings," "lord of lords," "hallelujah, hallelujah"—where everything is a D. We have accented "ha," we have accented "le," we have accented "lu," and after two electrifying beats of silence, Handel

EXAMPLE 15

[continued]

EXAMPLE 15 [continued]

gives us a glorious, majestic, concluding Amen that finally accents "jah"—"Hal-le-lu-JAH." "The kingdom of this world" has become "the kingdom of our Lord." The transformation is complete.

The Business of Music

It can be tempting to look at the history of music as nothing more than the history of musical compositions. As the purely internal story of how the musical language evolved over time without reference to external realities like audiences, patrons, commissioners, and publishers. However, music is more than just pure sound. It is also a concrete human activity rooted in the real world, and no form better illustrates the oftentimes complex interplay between art and commerce than the Baroque oratorio.

If you look at the development of classical music over its history, one of the most significant, overarching trends is the gradual democratization of audiences. An art form initially available to only a small, privileged segment of society in a few cultural centers has become available today, through the aid of recordings and the Internet, to nearly everyone nearly everywhere. What for centuries had been an elite, members-only private party has now been opened up to the global village, and each step along this path of democratization has transformed the lives and music of composers in significant ways. As I mentioned earlier, after coming to London, Handel spent thirty-five years composing, conducting, and producing Italian opera. It was no coincidence that the company that first engaged him, the Royal Academy of Music, had been organized by about sixty wealthy noblemen. Presenting Italian opera to the London public was fundamentally an elite, aristocratic affair. The average audience member in Handel's time probably understood no more Italian than audiences at the Metropolitan Opera did in the days before subtitles, but listening to opera in a foreign language had the same kind of snob appeal then that it does today. In addition, opera plots based on classical mythology and ancient history were designed for upper-class audiences who at least felt compelled to pretend to be acquainted with these subjects, though once again, the pretense was probably far greater than the reality.

However, opera was really the first form of public music that began to have a place in the audience for the nonaristocratic middle class, and they were growing tired of Italian opera, sung in a language they didn't understand with subject matter they knew nothing about. The London audiences felt ignorant and left out, and as the extraordinary popular success of John Gay's *The Beggar's Opera* in 1728 made abundantly clear, they wanted to hear music in English. To put it as simply as possible, if the audience for Italian opera in London had not dried up, and if Handel's own company had not failed, he would never have "invented" the oratorio. It was financial necessity far more than artistic conviction that led him to the form. It made economic sense. An oratorio, which used no sets or costumes, was vastly cheaper to produce than a fully staged opera. The middle-class public wanted to hear music in English about subject matter that they were familiar with, which in eighteenth-century London meant stories from the Bible. Handel, unlike Bach, had the temperament and the ability to adapt his musical style to the needs of this new middle-class public whose changing tastes would shape musical developments to a greater and greater extent in the years to come. Musically speaking, Handel's oratorios were really nothing more than Baroque operas on sacred subjects presented in concert rather than on the stage, but it was Handel's understanding of the new economic relationship between the independent composer/businessman and the emerging, middle-class public that made him not only a success in his own time but a harbinger of the future.

[4]

Franz Joseph Haydn
(1732–1809)
String Quartet, Op. 76, No. 1, Movement 3

Today there is but one music in all of Europe . . . this universal language of our continent.

—MICHEL CHABANON, 1785

Toward a Universal Language

If it is true, as the French theorist Michel Chabanon stated, that by the end of the eighteenth century there was "but one music in all of Europe" and it was the "universal language" of the continent, no one played a larger role in creating that "one music" than Franz Joseph Haydn. As the High Baroque style gradually gave way in the third quarter of the century to what has been called the pre-Classical or Rococo style, the musical scene in Europe was filled with a bewildering variety of national and local styles. French music was different from German music, and Italy alone had several different regional styles of music. Haydn's central role in the creation of a universal, European, Classical-period style is one of his greatest achievements, and it is against the background of this universal style that his music needs to be understood.

When Haydn began writing string quartets and symphonies in the 1760s (only a decade after Bach's death), there were no established formal or procedural norms for these genres, simply the diverse solutions of individual composers. By 1780, however, Haydn had created models that would serve as the basis and foundation for everything that Mozart and Beethoven would ultimately accomplish. The universality of the Viennese Classical style that Haydn helped create, as the 1785 quotation that opens this chapter indicates, was recognized at the time, and its widespread acceptance is an essential ingredient in understanding Haydn's music and its relationship to his audience.

Though it is rarely conscious on the part of its creator, every work of art from the simplest popular entertainment to the most complex work of modernist poetry or avant-garde music embeds in its content a belief about who its audience is and what they will or will not be able to follow. When Haydn wrote the G-Major String Quartet, op. 76, no. 1, in 1796, he was engaged in a dialogue with an audience that had a vast body of knowledge and experience with what had become, thanks to Haydn, a well-established genre. It should be mentioned that the principal "audience" for a Haydn string quartet in the eighteenth century was not a seated, ticket-buying public in a concert hall as it is today but rather the performers (usually amateurs) themselves. However, even the listeners who might have heard these quartets in a salon or at a private concert would almost certainly have played music themselves and would have heard or played other string quartets written by a wide range of composers. Since the G-Major Quartet was one of Haydn's late-period works, his audience had probably played or heard several of his previous quartets as well. Because of this extensive shared context, an extraordinarily sophisticated, witty conversation could take place. Put simply, an audience's knowledge of music and experience with other quartets determined the kind of quartet a composer could write and whether or not it would be understood—whether it would be a monologue or a dialogue—and Haydn's great achievement was to have established a universal language within which the remarkable conversation of a piece like the G-Major Quartet could take place.

This quartet belongs to a group of six quartets known collectively as the *Erdödy Quartets*, named after Count Joseph Erdödy, who commissioned the works. It was composed in 1796, shortly after Haydn's return from the second of his legendary trips to London, where his twelve *London* symphonies had established him as the most famous composer in all of Europe, hailed by the British press as "the greatest composer in the world." The quartet represents Haydn at the peak of his powers and the peak of his fame, and it is a superb example of his sophisticated, witty, unpredictable art.

Op. 76, No. 1, Movement 3: Constraint and Freedom II

One of the most impressive aspects of Haydn's achievements as a composer is the sheer volume of work he created. Though it is impossible to establish exactly how many pieces he wrote, scholars have provisionally authenticated 106 symphonies and 68 string quartets alone, not to mention 60 piano sonatas, between 20 and 25 operas, and 4 oratorios, as well as countless overtures, concertos, serenades, chamber works, cantatas, and Masses. Yet as remarkable as this prodigious output is, what is more remarkable is its variety, even within forms that might at first glance appear to be similar. If you look, for example, at Haydn's last 14 string quartets and 12 symphonies, their basic structure seems to be virtually identical. All 26 pieces are in four movements, begin and end with quick movements, and have a slow movement and a minuet in between. On rare occasions, the slow movement and minuet may reverse positions, or the opening movement may begin with a slow introduction, but otherwise the fundamental plans are almost indistinguishable. Though it might seem that the rigidity of this formula would lead to predictability and uniformity, for Haydn the effect is precisely the opposite. All 12 *London* symphonies may have the same basic external structure, yet each work is a one-of-a-kind version of that structure. In fact, it is the very uniformity and predictability of Haydn's forms that create the patterns and expectations that his richly subversive art continually undermines. In chapter 2, I mentioned Stravinsky's provocative idea that constraint in art produces freedom. Though in a very different way than it was for Bach, freedom within constraint is also the essence of Haydn's art, and there is no better place to see this in action than in the most "constrained" form in the Classical period—the minuet and trio.

The minuet and trio was the closest the Classical period came to a fixed form. As with a sonnet or a haiku, the externals of the form were fixed. A performer or a listener came to a minuet with an enormous set of expectations as to how the movement would unfold. In terms of tempo and meter, they expected to hear a movement in moderately fast, three-quarter time (though the tempo gradually sped up as the century progressed). They expected the movement to fall into three distinct sections. The first section, called the minuet, would be in two parts, with both parts repeated. The middle section, called the trio, would also be in two parts, with both parts repeated, and then the whole opening section would return without repeats. Minuet-trio-minuet. ABA for short.

If ever a form were constrained, and surrounded by "obstacles" to creativity, it would seem to be the Classical-period minuet. Yet for Haydn this very constraint was the source of his creative freedom. It was *because of*, not in spite of, this rigid, predictable formula that Haydn was able to create literally hundreds of utterly surprising, unique versions of the formula. The clearer the expectations of the listener, the greater the opportunity for manipulating those expectations, and Haydn's subversion begins with the extraordinary opening phrase of the G-Major Quartet's minuet.

EXAMPLE 1

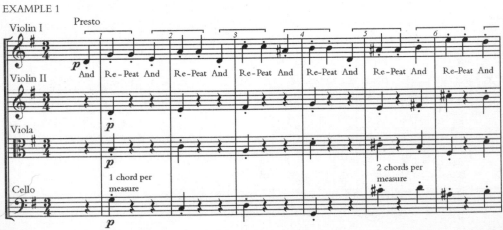

[continued]

EXAMPLE 1 [continued]

[continued]

EXAMPLE 1 [continued]

Part 1: To Be "Surprising in Convincing Ways"

Nearly all of Haydn's minuets have some "sticky" idea that unifies the movement, and this minuet's idea can be seen clearly by looking at the first two melody notes in each of the opening measures of the piece. Every measure begins with two repeated notes preceded by a pickup note from the previous measure, a three-note idea I will call "And Re-peat." In fact, if you look quickly through the entire minuet, you will see that thirty-three of its first forty measures begin with two repeated notes. Not only is Haydn's "field of action" limited by the external requirements of the minuet form, it is also constrained by the far more restrictive obstacle of each measure's having to begin with two repeated notes. However, it is the very rigidity of this framework that gives Haydn his creative freedom and allows him to develop an entire minuet out of variations on this one simple three-note idea.

Haydn's extraordinary compositional ingenuity is rooted in his ability to quickly both create and thwart patterns and expectations. The opening four-measures of this piece take less than three seconds to play; however, by the time they are completed, we already have a pattern and an expectation. A four-measure idea based on "And Re-peat" leads us to expect another one, but everything about the phrase that follows is a shock.

First of all, it is not a four-measure phrase at all, but a six-measure phrase. If I simply eliminate measures 7 and 8, you can hear the four-measure phrase that "should" have followed.

EXAMPLE 2

What happens instead is quintessential Haydn. On the most obvious surface level, the key dramatic moment in the phrase is the shocking switch to *fortissimo* in measure 8. Haydn is all about startling events like this; however, there is something much wittier and more sophisticated going on here than simply the shock of playing loud, fast eighth notes after seven quiet measures of quarter notes. First of all, the moment has been beautifully prepared in the cello part, which has gradually been speeding up, from one note per measure in measures 1 through 4, to two per measure in measures 5 and 6, then three in measure 7, leading finally to five per measure in the *fortissimo* bar. In addition, the *fortissimo* has been prepared melodically as well. Though the melody in measure 8 sounds and feels new because of its fast notes, it is really just a decoration of "And Re-peat." B-B-A becomes BB-BB-A. E. M. Forster said that "a rounded character in fiction must be surprising in convincing ways," and the preparation for this moment has been made so carefully that it sounds both surprising and convincing.

Part 2: Drama vs. Rhetoric

Though it is true that one of Haydn's lasting legacies to Mozart and Beethoven was the creation of a basic structure for the Classical-period sonata, string quartet, and symphony, perhaps equally important was his development of a fundamental way of working with a musical idea that lay at the center of all of these forms. This entire minuet is driven by the continual repetition, variation, expansion, and development of a single, tiny, motivic kernel: the three-note idea, "And Re-peat." This technique of breaking down a piece's thematic material into small units and dramatically developing these motives as the key engine behind a piece's musical "plot" would become fundamental to the way composers approached their material for the next two hundred years. Though there might seem to be some surface similarities to Bach's technique, an invention or a fugue explores the possibilities of a single musical idea in a rhetorical way. Haydn's exploration of a motive's possibilities, however, is inherently dramatic, and the second half of this minuet is a perfect example of this new Classical-period aesthetic.

Stravinsky said that the key to creativity is observation: noticing the possibilities right in front of your nose. Because this first section of the minuet ends while we are still recovering from the shock of the *fortissimo*, we barely notice the final notes of the phrase. But Haydn notices everything. The last two measures of the phrase (measure 9 and 10) actually contain the only other melodic idea in the piece— an idea that will be instantly recognizable whenever it occurs because it contains the sole measure in the minuet that *does not* begin with two repeated notes. I will call the whole six-note idea (beginning on the last note of measure 8) "And Scale Down and Re-peat."

The second section of the minuet begins by stringing together four versions of the opening idea to make a new shape—a rising scale over repeated D's in the cello (measures 11 through 14). This is a classic example of the kind of freedom possible within music of constraint. Each of the four measures is a version of "And Re-peat," yet when it is rearranged like this into a rising scale over a single repeated note in the cello and shifted into a minor key, the effect is dramatically different. This is no longer the rhetorical exploration of a Bach "invention" but rather the dramatic exploration and transformation of a Classical-period motive. This is the stuff of a novel, not an essay.

Then, suddenly, after four measures of "And Re-peat," Haydn begins to work with the seemingly insignificant ending of Part 1, "And Scale Down and Re-peat," now played *legato* (connected), not *staccato* (short and separated) as before, and shifted into a minor key (measures 15 through 18). Discovering that something that initially seemed to be an inconsequential detail, like this little closing figure, is in fact an essential element of the piece's material is once again quintessential Haydn. We never know in a piece of Haydn's what material will ultimately turn out to be important or what will turn out to be unimportant. A melody that initially seemed to be the main theme of a movement might eventually disappear from the musical conversation entirely, while a seemingly insignificant accompaniment, trill, or scale might become the central topic of the piece. These kinds of discoveries are always dramatic, and they are utterly dependent on audience expectations. Only in a style in which audiences have learned to immediately sense what is important and significant can these expectations be thwarted and manipulated in such striking ways. The continuous, uniform flow of a Baroque minuet could never provide the kind of aesthetic shock that is at the heart of the next phrase of Haydn's minuet.

Up until measure 18, the motion of the piece has been continuous. There have been no pauses in the melody (no rests), and every group of repeated notes has been preceded by a pickup note (the "And" before "Re-peat"). Then in measure 18, Haydn suddenly reduces the motive to its essence—just the two repeated notes—by removing the pickup note. "And Re-peat" becomes just "Re-peat . . . Re-peat . . . Re-peat." However, these two repeated notes are not just the essence of the opening motive; they are the essence of the entire piece, since "Re-peat" is what the piece's two ideas have in common. As if this is not enough to pay attention to, at the same time, the cello (measure 19) adds a pickup note to the single D's of measures 11 through 14 ("And Re") on the way back to the three-note idea that began the piece: "And Re-peat."

We are now at the dramatic center of the piece (measures 20 through 23). The melody has "Re-peat . . . Re-peat . . .Re-peat" but can't find its pickup note. The cello has "And Re . . . "And Re . . . And Re" but can't find "-peat." The music gets softer, the listener edges forward in his seat, and then in a fantastic stroke, the violin takes the cello's upbeat ("And Re-," D–D), alters its second note (D–G), and adds a third note to return to the opening melody (D–G–G). "And Re" has found "-peat."

The Return

This kind of fantastic moment is utterly typical of Haydn, and it is dramatic in a way that was new in its time. Many Baroque pieces have returns to the opening melody, but they are not dramatic like this. Baroque returns are grammatical, not theatrical. In a Classical-period piece, whether it be a sonata, a symphony, a quartet, or an opera aria, the return to the opening theme is always a structurally dramatic moment: a return "home" after a journey "away." In Haydn's minuet, everything works together—harmonically, motivically, and structurally—to articulate this central, form-defining moment, and the release that the listener feels at this moment of return is at the core of the Classical-period aesthetic.

In a piece of Haydn's, what comes after this moment of return is nearly always wildly unpredictable. In the music of other Classical-period composers, including Mozart and Beethoven, returns, or *recapitulations,** often largely involve simply repeating music heard earlier with essential material played outside the home key transposed back to the home key. Haydn's recapitulations, however, are nearly always surprising and revelatory. Material that seemed to be important is often eliminated, insignificant material gets expanded, sections return in an unusual order, new music is inserted—the listener never knows what will come next. Even a "simple" minuet like this one has a return of its opening section that is filled with surprises.

As I already mentioned, Haydn's extraordinary compositional ingenuity is rooted in his ability to both create and thwart patterns and expectations. The opening four measures of the piece return unaltered in measures 23 through 26, luring us into believing that the rest of the phrase will return unaltered as well; however, everything that follows is a complete surprise. Suddenly, the opening tune goes down into the cello underneath a brand-new melody in the violins with a rhythm not heard anywhere else in the movement (measures 27 through 30). And then, more quintessential Haydn. Out of nowhere, he simply invents three new measures of "And Re-peat" and stops dead (measures 31 through 33). The silence—the only actual pause in the entire movement—is fantastic and utterly unexpected. So many of Haydn's greatest moments are dramatic silences like this. Just when we are completely lost, on the brink of giving up hope that we will ever return to music we know, the *fortissimo* eighth notes return with a shock and seem to end the piece in measure 38 with the same music that ended section 1, now in the home key. A perfectly symmetrical and satisfying conclusion. Minuet over. But not quite! In a final touch that almost defines Haydn, just as the audience is metaphorically getting ready to applaud after the resounding *fortissimo* ending in measure 38, two witty, soft measures of "Re-peat, Re-peat" add an extra, surprise ending almost as

an afterthought. And as a bonus for the listener with a superb memory, these final three measures are actually a quotation of the three chords that opened the quartet two movements earlier (example 3). If ever a gesture could be called "Haydnesque," it is this ending. It is the essence of the Classical style in all its glory. "Surprising in a convincing way."

EXAMPLE 3

The Trio

The middle section, or trio, of a Classical-period minuet and trio is customarily in the same two-repeat form as the minuet, though it tends to be simpler in texture and content. For Haydn, however, what can seem simple at first hearing is often subtler than it appears,

EXAMPLE 4

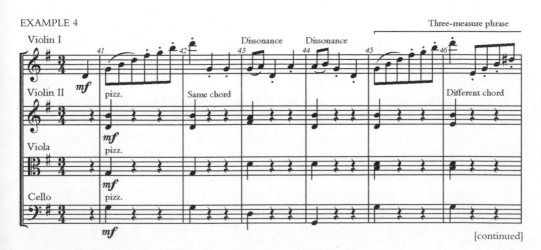

[continued]

EXAMPLE 4 [continued]

and I will use just the opening portion of this trio to demonstrate the principles behind the entire section.

Though we tend to make hard-and-fast distinctions today between serious and popular music, one of Haydn's great achievements was to create a style that effortlessly fused the two without making any artistic concessions, and the opening of this trio is a perfect example. Initially, it sounds like the music a peasant fiddler might play in a pub, and the plucked accompaniment and folklike dissonances (measures 43 and 44) perfectly capture the popular feel. However, if you listen closely, there are subtleties everywhere. For example, though the first two measures of the trio repeat the same chord, instead of copying the opening and again repeating the same chord in measures 45 and 46, Haydn beautifully changes the second chord. He then writes only one more measure in the unit (measure 47), making this a subtly irregular three-measure phrase (measures 45 through 47). Finally, after plucking only one chord per measure in the accompaniment for the whole opening of the phrase, he speeds up to three plucks per measure in measure 48 for two measures to elegantly vary the pulse and push to the cadence. In addition, this last unit is a wonderfully awkward five-measure unit, not a square four-measure unit like the Kapilow version in example 5.

The extra measure makes the phrase land with a witty, peasantlike thud on the final D of the melody, and the awkwardness of this final note is increased by the huge leap down in the first violin. But what makes all of this so "Haydnesque" is that when you combine the irregular three-measure phrase (measures 45 through 47) with this irregular five-measure phrase (measures 48 through 52), you get the most regular unit in all of Classical-period music—an eight-bar phrase! What sounds utterly irregular and surprising going forward

EXAMPLE 5

turns out to be utterly regular retrospectively. Nothing in Haydn is ever what it seems. The regular is irregular, the irregular regular. Once again, this is music that is "surprising in convincing ways."

Constraint and Freedom III

I mentioned that for Haydn, constraint was the source of his creative freedom, and this was as true of his life as it was of his music. Haydn was the last eminent composer to live happily under the old patronage system. His 1761 employment contract with Prince Paul Anton Esterhazy, head of one of the wealthiest and most powerful Hungarian noble families, reads like the contract of a servant. It spells out the clothing Haydn was to wear, his attitude and behavior, and every detail of his duties, including twice-daily appearances in the prince's antechamber to hear his Serene Highness's musical wishes. Not only did Haydn have to compose whatever music the prince wished (a requirement that ultimately forced Haydn to compose more than two hundred trios for the prince's favorite instrument, the baryton), he was not permitted to sell or give away any of his own compositions, nor was he allowed to compose for anyone other than the prince. Though this situation was eventually relaxed, Haydn still spent more than thirty years employed by the Esterhazys. Even after he received a taste of the possibilities of the freelance composer's life during his trips to London in the 1790s, when he returned to Vienna, he resumed his service with the Esterhazy family.

Though today this kind of rigidly regulated life within the old-fashioned patronage system might seem to be the definition of a life of "constraint," Haydn clearly felt it to be the source of his creative freedom. In a famous quotation, he said,

> My prince was pleased with all my work, I was commended, and as conductor of an orchestra I could make experiments, observe what strengthened and what weakened an effect and thereupon improve, substitute, omit, and try new things; I was cut off from the world, there was no one around to mislead and harass me, and so I was forced to become original.

Few composers' lives have been as externally boring as Haydn's, yet his daily routine freed him, as Stravinsky might have said, of the "chains that shackle the spirit." The days with Esterhazy were as similar to one another as the external plans of his symphonies and quartets, yet within this surface similarity there was astonishing variety, vitality, and surprise. In a Stravinsky-like manner, within his "narrowly limited field of action," surrounded by obstacles, both musically and personally, Haydn found extraordinary creative freedom. Though today Haydn has become something of a connoisseur's composer, clearly unable to compete at the box office with Beethoven or Mozart, when this quartet was written in 1796, Haydn was as famous as any composer has ever been. His music was not only popular with the general public but respected by the musical community.

In an interesting, fundamental way, despite a lifetime spent amid the wealth and privilege of the Esterhazys, Haydn wrote music that is deeply democratic. So often, his musical topics aren't elegantly crafted, exquisite, aristocratic melodies like Mozart's, but rather trivial bits of daily, workaday musical life—a simple scale or a group of repeated notes. Yet these ordinary ideas develop extraordinary life and vitality in Haydn's hands, as he somehow builds a dazzlingly witty, sophisticated musical universe out of insignificant basic building blocks. Nothing and no one in life, Haydn's music teaches us, is insignificant if we listen closely enough. In a quotation Haydn would have loved, Mark Twain said, "There was never yet an uninteresting life. . . . Inside of the dullest exterior there is a drama, a comedy, and a tragedy." Haydn couldn't have said it better himself.

[5]

Wolfgang Amadeus Mozart
(1756–1791)
"Dove Sono" from
The Marriage of Figaro

A world that has produced a Mozart is a world worth saving.

—FRANZ SCHUBERT

From Dramatic Sentiment
to Dramatic Action

Though Haydn and Mozart were the two outstanding composers of the late eighteenth century, their lives and temperaments could not have been more different. Mozart, of course, was the most famous child prodigy in the history of Western music. He started composing simple keyboard pieces at age five, progressed to violin sonatas and orchestral music at six and seven, and wrote his first symphony at age nine. In addition to being a precocious genius as a composer, he was also a virtuoso performer, thoroughly cosmopolitan, and an elegant lover of high society. Haydn, on the other hand, developed slowly as a composer, and was a competent but not virtuosic performer who lived a quiet, routine life on the remote Esterhazy estate, where he was as proficient at handling the practical details of daily life as Mozart was inept.

The two composers had not only different personalities but different compositional strengths as well. Though they both wrote symphonies and chamber works that are among the greatest in the repertoire, the brilliance of Mozart's operas and concertos was unmatched by Haydn or any other contemporary composer. Reading Mozart's letters, it quickly becomes clear that for him opera was the single most important and rewarding of all his creative endeavors. He was an astounding musical dramatist, and his theatrical gift was the key to his success in both opera and concerto: two genres that deal on the most fundamental level with the dramatic opposition and balance of soloists and orchestra.

As we have seen in earlier chapters, the Baroque style was fully capable of powerful dramatic expression of a particular kind. As Charles Rosen puts it, "Dramatic expression, limited to the rendering of a sentiment or of a significant theatrical moment of crisis . . . had already found musical form in the High Baroque." But what Mozart was striving for was not simply the expression of a single, static emotional state or affect, but rather the expression of dramatic action. Zerlina must try to resist Don Giovanni while secretly wanting to surrender. When confronted by her husband's infidelity, the Countess must move from playfulness through anger and humiliation to nostalgia, resolve, and a commitment to action. Mozart's operas replaced the Baroque expression of a single emotion with a continually evolving dramatic process. The seamless, uniform flow of the Baroque period was supplanted by a Classical style of clearly articulated dramatic events. As Rosen puts it succinctly, "Dramatic sentiment was replaced by dramatic action."

The Marriage of Figaro

Mozart was the master of this new kind of dramatic action, and there is no better example of his theatrical genius than *The Marriage of Figaro*. Written in 1786, *The Marriage of Figaro* was the first of Mozart's three great Italian operas written to librettos by Lorenzo Da Ponte. (*Don Giovanni*, 1787, and *Così fan Tutte*, 1790, were the other two.) The opera was only moderately successful in Vienna, where it was premiered, but it was given a wildly enthusiastic reception in Prague that same year, leading to a commission for *Don Giovanni* for the following season. Though the *Figaro* libretto is filled with stock situations and standard characters, Mozart's penetrating psychological insight turns these clichéd types into poignantly human, three-dimensional individuals, and one of the most moving examples is the Countess's famous third-act recitative and aria, "Dove sono i bei momenti?" ("Where are the lovely moments?").

The incredibly complex plot begins as Figaro, the valet to Count Almaviva, is making preparations to marry Susanna, the Countess's chambermaid. The Count, however, has his eye on Susanna himself and hopes that by promising her a dowry he can get her to yield to the droit du seigneur and obtain her favors in secret. The young and virtuous Susanna feels compelled to tell both Figaro and the Countess about the Count's intentions, and the three decide to try to foil the Count's plan. They decide that Susanna will pretend to agree to an assignation with the Count, but that the Countess will appear in her place instead. As the Act III scene begins, the Countess is waiting to find out if the Count has taken the bait and agreed to the meeting.

EXAMPLE 1

[continued]

EXAMPLE 1 [continued]

Recitative

As is so often the case in Mozart's operas, a *recitative** precedes the actual aria, and the dramatic action begins with the first phrase. I mentioned earlier that great composers don't set words to music, they set the emotions behind the words, and here every orchestral detail captures some emotional nuance or aspect of the Countess's character hidden beneath her words. Mozart composes what she is thinking and feeling, not what she is saying.

The opening line of text reads "E Susanna non vien?" ("And Susanna hasn't come?"), and the very first chord in the harpsichord already gives us a subtle sense of the Countess's anxiety. Instead of beginning the recitative with a normal, firmly grounded chord (example 2A), Mozart begins with an uncertain, anxious chord—an inversion (example 2B).

EXAMPLE 2A   EXAMPLE 2B

After the Countess utters her opening line, the strings enter with tentative music that immediately shifts key, perfectly depicting her anxiety over the fact that Susanna hasn't arrived (measure 2). The text that follows seems relatively straightforward: "Sono ansiosa di saper, come il Conte accolse la proposta!" ("I'm anxious to know how the Count took the proposition!") Surely, it seems, Mozart should simply continue with more anxious music. However, the orchestral fragment in measure 4 hints at a psychological side to the Countess that is in no way apparent in the words. In spite of her anxiety over the whole situation, the wonderful, quick figure in the strings shows her girlish pleasure in their little scheme. She is fearful, yet in Mozart's reading, a part of her is also enjoying the prospect of trapping her unfaithful husband.

Mozart then takes this a step further and actually subverts Da Ponte's text. The libretto says, "Alquanto ardito il progetto mi par" ("The plan seems to me a little rash"). However, the "girlish-pleasure" figure repeats itself higher and with more intensity (measure 6). Though her conscious mind might think that the plan is rash, the Countess is getting caught up in the fun of it in spite of herself, and as the recitative progresses, both the music and her emotions change with lightning speed. There is in fact danger in this plot, and in the very next line, she acknowledges the reality of who she is dealing with—"e ad uno sposo sì vivace e geloso!" ("and against such a quick and jealous husband!").

Suddenly her lighthearted, girlish music is interrupted by two melodramatic, *opera-seria** chords ("bum-bum," measure 8). As her pulse begins to quicken, the tempo speeds up to *allegretto,* and her "girlish-pleasure" figure is now harmonized with turbulent, dissonant chords in a minor key that reflect her fears over what might happen. However, an instant later, her mood shifts again, as she tries to calm herself down: "Ma che mal c'è?" ("But what harm is there in it?") Once again the music perfectly captures this moment as the return to a slower tempo and a more soothing string figure *is* the Countess trying to calm herself down (measure 10). Every emotional nuance and psychological shift is matched by the music. This is music as dramatic action, not music as dramatic sentiment.

The Moment of Truth

Throughout the recitative, Mozart continues to bring the Countess's kaleidoscopic mood swings to life with remarkable subtlety. As she quickly recounts the plan to herself—she simply wants to exchange clothes with Susanna under cover of night—her attempts to ease her anxiety are beautifully depicted by repeating the "calming-herself-down" figure of measure 10 three times, each time lower in pitch.

Then suddenly, as if speaking her plan out loud has forced her to recognize the truth of her situation, all pretense vanishes. Over two dissonant, accented melodramatic chords, she angrily and bitterly acknowledges the depths to which she has fallen. "Oh cielo! A qual umil stato fatale io son ridotta da un consorte crudel!" ("Oh heaven! What a fatal comedown I'm reduced to by a cruel husband!") As she lists each of her husband's offenses—his infidelity, his jealousy, and his rage ("d'infedeltà, di gelosia, di sdegno")—the music perfectly captures her rising anger as both the vocal line and the interrupting chords in the strings rise higher and higher in pitch.

The final five measures of this recitative are a stunning example of

EXAMPLE 3

[continued]

EXAMPLE 3 [continued]

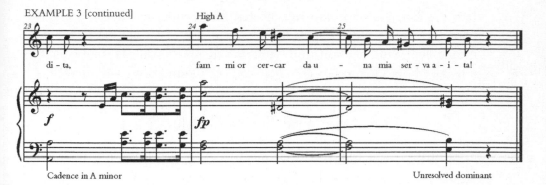

the dramatic power of Mozart's operatic language. The Countess's anger has caused both the voice part and the orchestra part to rise in pitch from measure 19 to measure 20. At the height of her anger, she pauses and sums up her entire marriage in three short fragments: "Prima amata, indi offesa, e alfin tradita" ("First beloved, then insulted, and at last betrayed"). The words "First beloved" force the Countess to mentally travel back in time to try to remember what her relationship with her husband was like when she was truly beloved. This memory momentarily allows her to leave the anger of the previous phrase behind as she plaintively floats a high F then poignantly descends a scale, while the strings, caught up in the memory as well, play three soft chords (measure 21). "Then insulted" instantly changes the mood to anger as the vocal line rises, and the three soft orchestral chords become loud and aggressive. The final fragment, "at last betrayed," finishes the survey of her relationship with an incredibly powerful orchestral cadence in A minor (note the striking low cello and bass notes in measure 23 marking the cadence).

This leads to three measures that almost define what makes Mozart's operas so great. Having finally faced and acknowledged her husband's betrayal, the Countess, in a moment of utter humiliation, leaps up to an extraordinary high A—the highest note of the entire recitative—to sing "fammi or cercar da una mia serva aita" ("you force me to seek help from one of my maids"). Though this high note can be a thrilling vocal moment, it has absolutely nothing to do with external, crowd-pleasing virtuosity. It is the intensity of her emotion that generates the register. The high note comes from the shame she feels at being forced to turn to her maid for help. It is not so much a vocal moment as it is a cry of pain. After the momentary outburst on the high note, the hushed cadence that ends the recitative is almost unbearably poignant.

It is the cadence of a woman who has finally shed her illusions and confronted the reality of lost love. The recitative ends unresolved harmonically because the situation is unresolved emotionally. Having honestly faced her circumstances, where can the Countess go from here?

The Aria: The Great Golden Past

One of the most standard ways of organizing an opera aria in the eighteenth century was to begin with a recitative; follow it with a slow, lyrical aria; and conclude with a fast, brilliant closing section. Though "Dove sono" follows this conventional three-part plan, each moment and section feels emotionally motivated, character-driven, and part of a surprising yet satisfying psychological journey. Having accepted the humiliating reality of her situation by the end of the recitative, the Countess temporarily withdraws from the pain of the present (the music of the recitative) into her memories of the past (the music of the aria). In an exquisite, magical moment, Mozart paints this nostalgic retreat into memory through an extremely subtle harmonic shift. I mentioned a moment ago that the recitative ends without harmonic resolution. The normal procedure would be to simply resolve this unresolved chord directly to an A-major chord to begin the aria like this:

EXAMPLE 4

This straightforward resolution would make for a smooth transition from the end of the recitative to the beginning of the aria, but Mozart is not interested in a smooth musical transition. He wants us to feel the Countess leaving reality behind and nostalgically drifting off into the world of the past. And so in a sublimely subtle harmonic shift, instead of resolving to A major, he resolves unexpectedly higher, to a surprising, ethereal C-major chord, like this:

EXAMPLE 5

Not only does the Countess's memory of the past have its own magical key, it has its own tempo (*andante*), continuous rhythm, lyrical singing, and orchestration, as woodwinds join the orchestra after the strings–only recitative to add the sweetness of nostalgia to the sonic palette. Every detail in this opening section is dramatically conceived. The woodwinds beautifully connect and color the vocal fragments (the second one higher and more intense than the first), the lovely *arpeggio** in the voice floats up to caress the word *dolcezza* (sweetness), and the fast oboe notes at the end of the first eight-measure phrase beautifully paint *piacer* (pleasure). The phrase starts to repeat for four measures (with added horns), but the mention of the Count's lying lips ("labbro menzogner") subtly throws the Countess and her music off course. Suddenly the melody stops repeating, dotted rhythms show her anger, and the symmetry of regular four-measure phrases is broken by two three-measure phrases (measures 38 through 43). However, Mozart's psychological insight again creates complexity nowhere apparent in the text. The mention of the Count's "lying lips" has momentarily allowed anger to disturb the Countess's reverie, but Mozart has her repeat the phrase, and the second time through, her angry dotted rhythms and rising vocal line vanish, replaced by a sweet, nostalgic, graceful descent and cadence as she remembers how she once felt about those lips.

Section Two: I Can't Get Him Out of My Mind

The setting of the text for the aria's middle section—"Perchè mai se in pianti e in pene per me tutto si cangiò, la memoria di quel bene dal mio sen non trapassò!" ("Why, if all is changed for me into tears and pain, has the memory of that goodness not vanished from my breast!")—is as dramatically subtle as the opening. The music shifts keys to G major (as if to begin the second section of a sonata) as the Countess shifts focus from her memories of the past to the tears and pain of the present, but right on the words "tears and pain," in the middle of measure 46, Mozart subtly shifts to minor in the vocal line to bring the text to life.

EXAMPLE 6

Then, as the thought sinks in, on the words "per me tutto si cangiò" ("for me all has changed"), this new, changed reality is reflected in the changed accompaniment, which now starts to move in quick rhythm for the first time in the piece (measure 49).

The section continues until it reaches a cadence and a brief pause, followed by a repeat of the opening music. The Countess repeats all of the aria's first phrase and seven measures of the second, but this time at the mention of the Count's lying lips the music stops right in the middle of the thought. This moment is another perfect example of Mozart's ability to combine form, text, and music into an indivisible, dramatic whole. The abrupt pause is not simply a musical event—chopping off a six-measure phrase after three measures—but a dramatic event as well. We literally get to watch the "lightbulb" go off in the Countess's mind. One line of thought (thinking about his lying lips) is interrupted by another thought (the possibility of winning him back), and the interrupted musical phrase perfectly conveys the interrupted thought, as the excitement of her new plan generates the new tempo and the final section of the piece.

EXAMPLE 7

He'll Change

As I mentioned earlier, though the basic structure of this aria is utterly conventional, every moment and every formal seam is psychologically motivated. Text, music, and drama are one. And once again, what is conveyed here is dramatic action, not dramatic sentiment. The whole concluding section expresses a single idea—the possibility of winning back the Count through a display of faithfulness—but we watch that idea develop in the Countess's mind, beginning during the silence in measure 77. First it is just a three-word fragment interrupted by orchestra chords—"Ah! se almen . . ." ("Ah! if only . . .") Then, another three-word fragment interrupted by orchestra chords—"la mia costanza" ("my faithfulness"). "Nel languire amando ognor" ("which still loves amid its suffering") brings a quick turn to minor (measure 80) and a more continuous vocal line to represent the suffering she still feels. But the hope of changing his heart—"di cangiar l'ingrato cor"—brings the music instantly back to major and a rhythmically flowing melody as the plan begins to solidify in her mind.

The exultant instrumental interlude that follows (measures 88 through 90) *is* her joy over this new plan, and the wonderful, character-filled decorations in measure 90 perfectly capture the hope she has begun to feel. However, excitement and hope are not static emotions for Mozart. Again, this is music of dramatic action, not dramatic sentiment. As the Countess gradually overcomes both her inner doubts and her anger at the suffering the Count has caused her, she becomes more and more confident of her plan, and Mozart conveys this shift in extraordinarily subtle ways. Though the Countess sings no new words in the final forty-five measures of the piece, Mozart eventually eliminates the first two text fragments—the fragments that refer to doubt and suffering—and for the last twenty-eight measures uses only the fragments that refer to hope. In addition, as these final words, "mi portasse una speranza di cangiar l'ingrato cor" ("could bring me the hope of changing that ungrateful heart"), are repeated over and over again, Mozart's dramatic approach changes. The musical feeling at the beginning of the section is uneasy. An edgy, sustained high A in measure 110 and a nervous, chromatic descent in measure 111 reveal a degree of inner turmoil still remaining in the Countess's mind. A repeat of the idea dispels some of the lingering doubt and leads to a more clear-cut cadence in measure 117. However, in the final section (measures 117 through 128), the Countess repeats the words as part of an ever-more-standard closing formula, with utterly conventional harmony and orchestral accompaniment. Order has been restored, doubts have been resolved, a plan of action is clear, and the final orchestral music allows the Countess to exit the scene with a sense of conviction, confidence, and certainty that seemed unimaginable when the scene began.

EXAMPLE 8

[continued]

EXAMPLE 8 [continued]

Things Are Not as Simple as You Think

In a famous letter to his father, Mozart describes his music as

> a happy medium between what is too easy and too difficult . . .
> very brilliant, pleasing to the ear, and natural, without being
> vapid. There are passages here and there from which connois-
> seurs alone can derive satisfaction, but these passages are written
> in such a way that the less learned cannot fail to be pleased,
> though without knowing why.

There is perhaps no other major composer whose music is so different from what it appears to be. So often, Mozart's music can seem
to be "merely beautiful." Yet if you listen to what lies beneath its surface perfection, nearly all of his greatest music is subtly subversive.

When the musical surface sounds simple, tuneful, and regular, the phrase structure is nearly always subtly irregular (like the three-measure phrases in "Dove sono," or the opening five-measure phrase of the *Haffner* Symphony). On the other hand, when the musical surface sounds jarring and disorienting, there is nearly always regularity underneath (as in the famous opening of the G-minor Symphony's development section). Mozart's music is like a sublimely balanced hologram —it is both simple and complicated at the same time—and grasping this contradiction is crucial to understanding not only his compositional style but his psychological approach to drama as well.

It is Mozart's ability to see so many different sides to human beings—even stereotypical characters in absurd situations—that is the basis of his operatic greatness. In *The Art of the Novel*, the brilliant Czech writer Milan Kundera wrote, "The novel's spirit is the spirit of complexity. Every novel says to the reader: 'Things are not as simple as you think.'" And every measure of Mozart's operas says this as well. *Don Giovanni* is both a tragedy *and* a comedy. The Don is a horrible blasphemer *and* a romantic hero. He is capable of brutally stabbing the Commendatore *and* singing exquisitely beautiful music to Zerlina. The Countess is enraged by her husband's infidelity and humiliated by the position in which she has been placed, but still, she wants nothing more than to find a way to win him back. She feels an enormous range of conflicting emotions—fear, jealousy, and anger; love, nostalgia, and hope—and in Mozart's reading, they are all true, and they are all given musical expression.

Some audiences and critics over the years have commented on what they find to be an unnerving sense of distance in Mozart's music: a kind of inhuman, almost-impersonal perfection. His manuscripts seem to have been dictated by God. There are almost no marks or revisions—a visual symbol of a compositional facility that borders on the miraculous. However, in spite of his uncanny, almost supernatural gifts, his musical vision is intensely human, yet human as seen from a kind of Shakespearean, God-like distance. Mozart sees everything and knows everything. He sees people's foibles and weaknesses yet also their generosity and compassion. He sees their arrogance and selfishness as well as their nobility and selflessness. And he brings an extraordinary, all-embracing sympathy to everyone, accepting them at their best and at their worst. Mozart's universe has room for us all.

[6]

Ludwig van Beethoven
(1770–1827)

Waldstein Sonata, Movement 1

Most of the great poets are impersonal, I am personal. . . . In my poems, all revolves around, concentrates in, radiates from myself. I have but one central figure, the general human personality typified in myself.

—WALT WHITMAN

To Make Music Personal

The relationship between an artist's life and his work is notoriously complex and indirect; however, there is something about Beethoven's music that compels us toward biography. It is possible to listen to the music of Mozart and Haydn without feeling that knowledge of their lives is essential to an understanding of their work, but Beethoven's music seems so direct, so immediate, so emotionally honest, and so personal that we feel compelled to find out who that person was. What Walt Whitman would later say of his own poetry might equally have been said by Beethoven: "In my [music], all revolves around, concentrates in, radiates from myself." Music as a mode of direct personal expression essentially begins with Beethoven. When he wrote in his Heiligenstadt Testament (his despairing, quasi-suicide letter to his brothers), "It seemed to me impossible to leave the world until I had brought forth all that I felt was *within me*" [my italics], the source of musical inspiration ("within me") was definitively located where it has resided ever since—inside the subjective heart and mind of the individual composer.

Placing subjectivity at the center of artistic expression was an enormous paradigm shift that ultimately affected every aspect of musical life. Beethoven's revolution was not only a revolution in terms of the content of the music he wrote, it was a revolution in whom that music was written for, how it was financed, and what its fundamental scope and purpose was. The idea of the composer as artistic genius, writing music that would live on into the future, began with Beethoven. When Beethoven said defiantly, "There are a thousand princes; there is only one Beethoven," the relationship between composer, patron, and public was changed forever.

As I mentioned earlier, Haydn was the last eminent composer to spend his life firmly ensconced in the old patronage system, working in a near-servant capacity for the Esterhazy family for some thirty years. Mozart began his career within this same patronage system in the service of the Archbishop of Salzburg, but left it behind (against his father's advice) when he became a freelance composer after moving to Vienna in 1781. However, in spite of considerable financial success (research has shown that stories of his desperate financial straits near the end of his life have been considerably exaggerated), Mozart never stopped looking for a permanent position. He lived outside of the old patronage system, yet continued to yearn for the security it represented.

Beethoven, however, was comfortable and successful within the new freelance world. His relationships with patrons were completely different from Mozart's and Haydn's. He saw himself as no one's servant, and he was received with respect and friendship at the highest levels of Viennese society. He treated his devoted patrons with complete independence and on occasion arrogance and rudeness. He once said, "It is well to mingle with aristocrats, but one must know how to impress them." And impress them he did, receiving expensive gifts, high fees for lessons, lucrative commissions, and, for a time, a yearly stipend from several wealthy individuals. Combining this income with the money he earned from concerts and publications left Beethoven quite well off financially, and this enabled him to write the music he wanted to write largely independent of the kinds of demands and deadlines that had been a regular part of previous composers' lives.

Though Beethoven was already quite successful in Vienna as a pianist/composer by 1800, the Beethoven revolution really began in earnest in 1802. October 1802 is the date of the famous Heiligenstadt Testament, and as the critic Joseph Kerman points out, shortly after Beethoven wrote this letter, something radically shifted in his compositional vocabulary. The period from 1802 to 1806 is one of the most exciting times in the history of Western music. During these years, Beethoven singlehandedly reinvented nearly all of the principal genres of the Classical style and created works that would fundamentally alter these genres forever. The *Eroica* Symphony, the *Waldstein* and *Appassionata* piano sonatas, the *Razumovsky* string quartets, the Fourth Piano Concerto, and the *Kreutzer* violin sonata were written during these years, and these pieces are all, to use Kerman's phrase, "pointed individuals" in ways that make Beethoven's earlier works in these genres seem almost neutral in comparison.

Before the Beethoven revolution, piano sonatas and string quartets were largely written for the extensive and very lucrative amateur market—for amateurs to play at home. But works like the *Razumovsky* quartets and the *Waldstein* and *Appassionata* sonatas were so difficult to play that they left not only most amateurs behind but most professionals as well. These works replaced the polite, private amateur world of "chamber music" with virtuosic, public music of symphonic scope and redefined the possibilities of these genres for the next two hundred years.

The *Waldstein* Sonata Exposition: Anything but "Pleasant"

Though today the Classical period is largely known through the music of its three most famous composers, for Beethoven's contemporaries the context for listening to works like the *Waldstein* Sonata was not only the music of the two other Classical-period geniuses, Mozart and Haydn, but also the workaday, everyday music of now largely forgotten composers like Clementi, Wölfl, and Cherubini. Since the piano sonata was largely the province of the amateur pianist, it was against the background of sonatas like Clementi's that most of

Beethoven's audience would probably have been playing on a daily basis that the opening page of the *Waldstein* Sonata would have been heard. To give you a sense of that context, here is the beginning of one of Clementi's popular piano sonatas, also in C-major, op. 29, no. 1.

EXAMPLE 1

These opening measures instantly give you a feeling for what the everyday world of the piano sonata was like for Beethoven's audience. Almost anyone with a year or two of piano lessons could have played this opening at sight, and the music is not only easy to play, it is easy to listen to as well. It makes no one's heart race. The rhythm lacks any real energy, and the dynamic contrasts, phrasing, and style could best be summed up by the word "pleasant." This is pleasant music that could be played effortlessly by young well-to-do girls and well-meaning amateurs for their private amusement or after dinner for friends and relatives.

To give a slightly fuller picture, here is another C-major piano sonata from the same general time period, by Haydn. The tempo is brighter, the music is more interesting, and notice for comparison to the *Waldstein* Sonata the way the opening tune is first played softly with sparse accompaniment and then repeated loudly with a more continuous left hand.

EXAMPLE 2

[continued]

EXAMPLE 2 [continued]

Now, keeping everything about these two pieces in mind—who could play them, the setting in which they might be played, their energy level, the demands they make on the listener, their fundamental keyboard sonority, and in particular their overall level of drama—listen to the opening thirteen measures of the *Waldstein* Sonata.

EXAMPLE 3

[continued]

EXAMPLE 3 [continued]

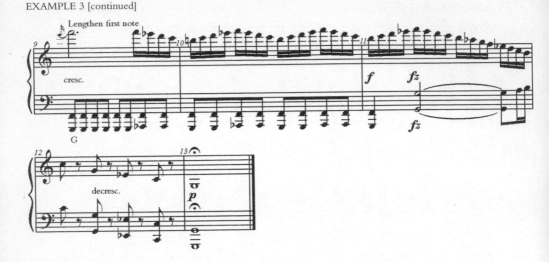

What is it that makes this opening so radical? First of all, the sonority is incredibly dramatic. Unlike the Clementi and Haydn sonatas, which are largely written in a "pleasant," neutral register in the middle of the keyboard, the *Waldstein* Sonata begins *pianissimo,* with thick, pulsing chords in the low register of the keyboard. In addition, though both the Clementi and Haydn sonatas begin with easily singable, memorable tunes, there isn't a single real "melody" in the entire *Waldstein* opening. Instead, there are three fragmentary ideas that in and of themselves could not be less interesting or more elementary. Idea 1 is a pulsing, block-chord idea that ultimately rises a *third** (see example 3), while ideas 2 and 3 are nothing more than rude "flicks." Flick 1 starts and ends on the same note, and flick 2, kicked off by an irritating *grace note,** descends a simple, five-note scale (see example 3). Beethoven is building his thematic universe here out of the most basic, insignificant elements of the style. To create an enormous, dramatic movement out of such primitive, unappealing, almost grotesque material is utterly unprecedented. Haydnesque wit and Mozartean elegance have been replaced by a new musical language with a completely new aesthetic purpose.

Contextual Travel

What happens next and the challenge of comprehending it for a modern listener goes to the heart of the whole problem of historical context. In the nineteenth century, people were obsessed with exotic travel to remote places like Tahiti, India, and Africa, yet for us in the twenty-first century who have traveled everywhere, both geographically and musically, it can be hard to recapture the nineteenth-century listener's sense of the exotic. To be specific, an audience listening to a piece of music in 1804 expected musical travel at the beginning of a piece to be conventional and local. Establishing a stable frame was crucial, and a composer rarely strayed far from "home" harmonically. The *tonic** and the *dominant** are the two chords or pillars that define a key—"home" in a piece of tonal music. The *Waldstein* Sonata begins in C major (the tonic), and it arrives on a G-major chord (the dominant) at the end of measure four. A standard continuation that remained in the home key might repeat the opening like this:

EXAMPLE 4

Perhaps somewhat more exotically, but still in the home key, a composer might have done this:

EXAMPLE 5

Five seconds into the piece, however, Beethoven travels to the musical equivalent of Tahiti (B-flat major) and replays the opening music in an utterly foreign key (measure 5, example 3)!

From here, things only get worse. Flick 2 turns minor (measure 8) and then gets distorted with a lengthened first note (measure 9). At the same time, the sonority becomes astonishing, with a huge distance between the left and right hands, each at the extreme ends of Beethoven's keyboard. The music gets louder and louder as the sonority gets more and more brutal until a dramatic *diminuendo* ends the first phrase with a theatrical pause on a soft unison.

No one had ever written an opening like this before, but though the surface of the music might sound confusing and radical, its underlying structure is actually logical and traditional. If you follow the bass line (the lowest voice) over the entire phrase, it clearly traces out a simple chromatic scale (a scale that moves from each note to the next nearest note on the keyboard) as it descends step by step from one pillar of the tonal universe to the other (C–B–B♭–A–A♭–G). From tonic to dominant, from C to G.

EXAMPLE 6

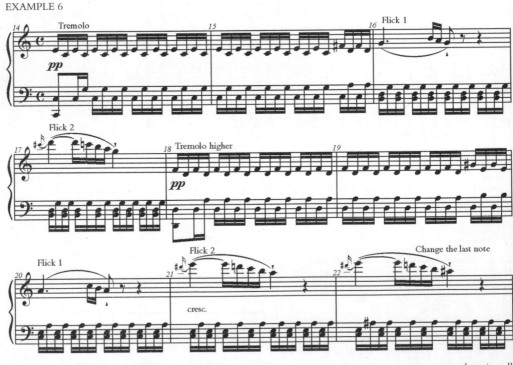

[continued]

EXAMPLE 6 [continued]

Though measure by measure we seem to be on a bewildering, exotic journey to Tahiti (remote keys), we have actually never left home (C major)! Going forward, everything is shocking and surprising. As we look backward, Beethoven's compelling logic becomes clear.

Beethoven's music was more extreme in every way than the music of any of his contemporaries. It was louder, faster, more intense, more dramatic, more virtuosic, more dynamically varied, more dissonant, more accented, and more violent. The Clementi and Haydn C-major sonatas ease us into their world, but the *Waldstein* Sonata grabs us by the throat and refuses to let go. When the first phrase ends at measure 13, we are desperate for relief, for order, and for balance, which in the Classical period means repetition. However, the repeat of the opening phrase is even more unnerving than the original version.

The pulsing chords that began the piece now become an even more propulsive tremolo (example 6, measure 14) followed by flick 1 and flick 2. But this time instead of going to Tahiti (*down* to B-flat), Beethoven goes to Asia (*up* to D in measure 18). And amazingly enough, once that gesture is complete, approximately thirty seconds into the piece, we have heard all the significant material of the first *theme group** of the sonata. As is so often the case in Beethoven's middle-period works, though the first movement as a whole is enormous, the exposition, or statement of essential materials, is brutally economical. Two phrases are all that is needed, and everything that follows is preparation for the second theme, which ultimately arrives in measure 35.

Preparation and Second Theme: "Are We There Yet?"

Though today we have grown familiar with Beethoven's heroic style, one of its radically new features was passages of preparation of staggering lengths. Put simply, Beethoven was willing to make his listeners wait longer for resolutions and arrivals than any previous composer, and these delays created unprecedented dramatic tension. Though the preparation for the *Waldstein* Sonata's second theme lasts only twelve measures (from measure 23 to measure 34), the complete lack of significant themes, the intensity created by the speeding up of the harmonic pacing in measures 27 and 28, and the brutally simple round in measures 31 through 34 all combine to make the arrival of the new theme in the unexpected key of E major seem like an enormous release.

In a Classical-period work, the movement away from the home key and the arrival at a second key is always a fundamentally dramatic event—a true movement "away"—that is dissonant on the larger level of the piece and must ultimately be resolved. Though a work by Bach might also move away from its home key and arrive at a second key, the effect is completely different. Bach's harmonic universe is far more fluid than Beethoven's, and this allows him to slide in and out of keys with much less drama and articulation. The cadences "away from home" in Bach's C-Major Two-part Invention are clearly marked, but they are no more than a momentary pause in the movement's continuous flow. However, in the *Waldstein* Sonata, the arrival of the second key is a clearly articulated, highly dramatic event that leads to an extended section in the new key. The texture changes completely, the rhythmic motion stops, and a new theme enters in the new key to underline this important structural moment.

Interestingly enough, though this choralelike second theme could not sound more different from the material of the opening, it is actually flick 2 with each note stretched out rhythmically.

EXAMPLE 7

This kind of subtle thematic connection contributes to the powerful feeling of inevitability in Beethoven's music—the sense that if we only listen closely enough, all the musical ideas in a work are related. The only other thematic idea in this remarkably compact exposition is again utterly elementary—a series of first-year-piano-student arpeggios played against a syncopated, repeated-note figure with both parts immediately switching hands.

EXAMPLE 8

One of the things that struck all of Beethoven's contemporaries was the unprecedented length of his pieces. The *Eroica* Symphony was nearly double the length of an average symphony, and enormous movements like the opening movement of the *Waldstein* Sonata stretched listeners' attention spans in completely new ways. However, in addition to the actual duration of his pieces, one of the elements that gives Beethoven's middle-period music such an enormous sense of breadth and expansiveness is his willingness to take the simplest harmonic progressions and expand them to unheard-of lengths. For example, all first-year harmony students learn a simple, three-chord formula as a way to lead to the close of a musical paragraph (example 9A). Beethoven, however, takes this simple formula and brutally hammers, *fortissimo*, at each of the first two chords twelve times in the left hand and then expands the resolution of the final chord as well, turning this simple cadence formula into a passage of enormous scope (example 9B).

EXAMPLE 9A

EXAMPLE 9B

[continued]

EXAMPLE 9B [continued]

A brief *coda** concludes the exposition, and its final figure finds its way back home from "Asia" to C major step-by-step in order to repeat the entire exposition. Unlike Mozart, who would surely have accomplished this return in one elegant surprise, Beethoven wants us to see the effort and feel the distance, as the ending figure needs three tries before it finds its way back home. Connection is always the product of human effort in Beethoven's universe. Nothing is hidden. We are meant to watch the process as it happens, and these relationships are visible on the surface of the music, audible to any listener.

EXAMPLE 10

Searching for Essences: Development—Section 1

The centerpiece of nearly all Beethoven sonata movements is their development section, and Beethoven's whole approach to development—how he transforms and varies a musical idea—is at the heart of the Beethoven revolution. The development section of the *Waldstein* Sonata begins with the movement's opening pulsing chords and then immediately starts working with the two flicks.

EXAMPLE 11

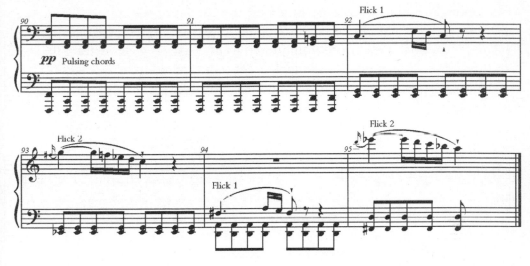

Though the core of Beethoven's developmental technique comes from Haydn, not only are Beethoven's development sections far longer and more dramatic than Haydn's, they are directed toward different aesthetic ends. For Beethoven, development is fundamentally about stripping away the inessential in order to discover the essential—the core meaning of a piece's basic material. Up to this point, each flick has lasted one measure (four beats). Suddenly the piece radically shifts gears and doubles the music's fundamental pulse, compressing both flicks into a single measure.

EXAMPLE 12

However, he is doing more here than simply creating intensity, excitement, and drama by doubling the pacing of the music. What Beethoven is really doing is stripping away the inessential to get at the essential. Flick 1 gets compressed to its essence by eliminating its lengthened first note, while flick 2 gets compressed to its essence by eliminating its grace note and tied first note.

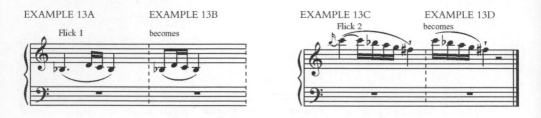

Once these ideas have been reduced to their essences, they can freely combine in new ways, as they do in measures 96 through 99. However, Beethoven takes this reduction one step further in measures 104 through 109. Suddenly, every fourth statement substitutes a single note for all of flick 1.

EXAMPLE 14

Reducing this key thematic material to a single half note, and having that one note "stand for" the idea, is what Beethoven's developments are all about, and as always, this connection is man-made, visible on the surface of the music, and audible to the listener.

Geometric Music: Sections 2 and 3

Having seemingly exhausted the possibilities of these two flicks, Beethoven starts to work on the "first-year-piano-student-arpeggio" idea in section two. After only one measure, however, its repeated-note figure is eliminated, and the idea evaporates into an essence—pure arpeggios. In the same way that a landscape painting by Cézanne focuses on the underlying geometric shapes of a scene and not on the details of each tree and leaf, Beethoven starts to be interested in big, geometric blocks of harmony without pretty, detailed musical surfaces. For thirty measures, Beethoven reduces the entire piece to pure harmony without any melodic content, working with the bold, broad strokes of a thick housepainter's brush, not Mozart's elegant, finely detailed paintbrush.

EXAMPLE 15

The passage that Beethoven struggled with the most in composing this development section and the one most characteristic of his heroic style is what musicians call the *retransition**—the passage that prepares for the return of the opening music. To give you a sense of what Beethoven's audiences expected at this moment, here is a typical Clementi retransition passage. It is not only short, it is anything but dramatic.

EXAMPLE 16

For a bit more context, below is a Haydn retransition. Though the music cleverly prepares the listener for a return in the wrong key, this feint is wittily rerouted in the fourth measure, and the return follows almost immediately.

EXAMPLE 17

The Way Back Home

Stage 1 of Beethoven's *Waldstein* retransition is fairly traditional, and after six measures we feel ready for the opening theme to return.

EXAMPLE 18

The next fourteen measures, however, are amazing. The left hand takes the ending of flick 2 and in an extraordinary moment of re-invention turns it into a rumble at the bottom of Beethoven's piano, going both down (measure 142) and up (measure 143).

EXAMPLE 19

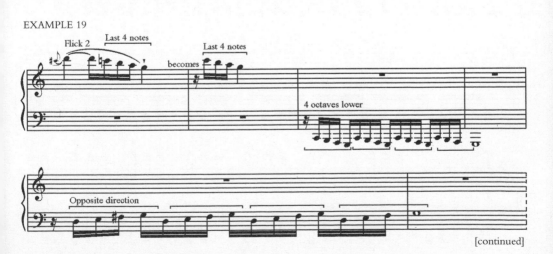

[continued]

EXAMPLE 19 [continued]

[continued]

EXAMPLE 19 [continued]

Then, while the left hand obsessively repeats this fragment over and over again, the right hand pulverizes the flicks into atomic nuclei rising higher and higher as the sonority gets harsher and harsher until an electrifying one-measure swoop at the extreme ends of the keyboard brings in the return of the opening theme to begin the recapitulation. No one had ever written music like this before, and these twenty thrilling measures of dramatic delay are what the Beethoven revolution was all about.

Recapitulation and Coda: Completing the Journey

The recapitulation neatly brings back all of the music of the exposition in order to contain and balance the radical energies unleashed by the piece so far. A short passage develops the dramatic pause of measures 12 and 13 and renders it "harmless."

EXAMPLE 20

[continued]

EXAMPLE 20 [continued]

In a new approach to the idea of compositional balance, the choralelike second theme that was originally heard a third above the home key is balanced by returning a third below the home key. It then turns to minor in order to return to the home key, and once again Beethoven shows us the connection step-by-step.

EXAMPLE 21

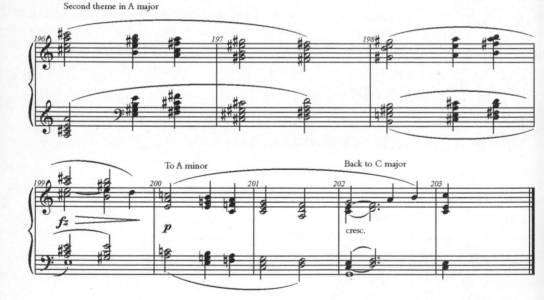

The coda's journey is an extraordinary one. It begins in the musical equivalent of Siberia, as far from the home key as possible—in the key of D-flat. For the first time, the bass line *rises* underneath the compressed flicks of the development section as Beethoven thrillingly finds a way back to the brink of the home key.

EXAMPLE 22

It will take twenty-three more amazing measures to finally resolve to C major, but while we wait, Beethoven gives us two last transformations of the opening material that are unbelievably ear-stretching. The original pulsing chords

EXAMPLE 23A

turn into this in the left hand.

EXAMPLE 23B

When this is combined with a new right hand, the original material is almost unrecognizable.

EXAMPLE 23C

As if all of this isn't eccentric enough, Beethoven then takes the little grace note that originally kicked off flick 2 and turns it into a huge, willfully awkward leap in the left hand that rises higher and higher to lead into a passage that Beethoven called a *cadenza** in the very first sketches of the piece as if he were writing a concerto, not a sonata.

EXAMPLE 24

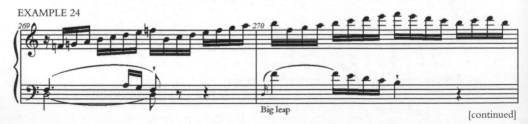

[continued]

EXAMPLE 24 [continued]

[continued]

EXAMPLE 24 [continued]

Finally, after thirty-five measures, the arrival of the choralelike second theme (measure 284) not only resolves the coda harmonically but also resolves the entire piece structurally, as we have been waiting to hear this theme in the home key (C major) for the whole movement. As is so often the case in Beethoven's music, once the essential compositional work of a piece is done, the ending is brutally abrupt. The opening, pulsing chords return, and a single eight-measure phrase sums up and rounds off all of the thematic content of the piece. The ending is as short as the movement is long, and the piece is over before we know it. The *Waldstein* Sonata's revolution is surprising and unpredictable until its final note.

EXAMPLE 25

[continued]

EXAMPLE 25 [continued]

"Only Connect"

"Only connect," wrote E. M. Forster, and he might well have been describing Beethoven's entire compositional approach. As early as 1829, the brilliant critic A. B. Marx sensed that connectedness and relatedness were at the heart of Beethoven's music when he proposed that "Beethoven composed each of his works according to a 'fundamental idea' that underpinned the connectedness, unity, and harmony of its apparently discordant features." Beethoven's compositional technique says in essence, "We look at the surface of things and see difference, yet the differences that separate us are superficial and illusory. What is fundamental is what is the same." And finding that fundamental connectedness and unity behind difference has become the essential work of the composition.

However, it was not only a new kind of compositional connection that Beethoven was interested in but a new kind of connection with the public as well—connection on the most profound, elemental level. For Beethoven, music as mere entertainment was insufficient. Composer, performer, and listener now became partners on a spiritual journey. In this new relationship, all parties agree to bring the best of themselves—their truest and deepest natures and their most profound listening—to a shared artistic experience. The concert hall becomes the place where we shed our superficial trappings and connect on the most serious, fundamental level. We leave behind our individual world of "me" and become part of a universal brotherhood of man—a Beethovenian world of "we."

Though his advancing deafness was devastating to Beethoven as a composer, it is clear that the isolation from humanity that this led to was almost as devastating as the deafness itself. In spite of his notoriously difficult personal relationships, Beethoven craved human contact and connection. There is something deeply poignant about the image of an aging Beethoven, more and more physically isolated from the world, desperately searching for a relatedness and connectedness in his music that was so heartbreakingly absent from his own difficult and troubled personal life.

It is impossible to study Beethoven's life and not be struck again and again by his extraordinary daily psychological struggles. To have created all that he did in the midst of his paranoia, hysteria, hallucinations, despair, and mental instability is an achievement almost as great as the music itself. Yet the more you delve into his life, the more you begin to sense that the power of his music is not in spite of this psychological torment but in response to it. Each calamitous occurrence—the onset of his deafness, the French occupation of Vienna, the suicide attempt of his nephew—seemed, after a period of crisis and withdrawal, to lead to major artistic steps forward. Beethoven not only faced and overcame every challenge; he seemed to use each challenge, and the internal processing of these challenges, as a spur to a deepening of his art.

Joseph Campbell says that "opportunities to find deeper powers within ourselves come when life seems most challenging. Negativism to the pain and ferocity of life is negativism to life itself. The warrior's approach is to say 'yes' to life: 'yes' to it all." Beethoven's music is the music of a spiritual warrior. It says yes to a life filled with pain, unhappiness, isolation, and struggle that you can feel and see in every scratched-out, passionately scrawled measure of his nearly illegible manuscripts. It says yes to the complete range of human emotions. To the beautiful and to the ugly. To the sublime and to the ordinary. It says, "Yes to life: yes to it all."

[7]

Franz Schubert
(1797–1828)
"Erlkönig"

———

Every exceptional individual has a certain mission that he is called to carry out.

—GOETHE

A Certain Mission

Nearly all encyclopedia and dictionary entries about Schubert call him "the greatest song composer in history." Though he was far more than that, the fact that being the greatest song writer in history might make him worthy of a place among the pantheon of the great composers is in itself a mark of his achievement. In the eighteenth century, major composers spent almost no time writing songs because the form was considered too unimportant and insignificant to merit their attention. Schubert's great accomplishment was to take this genre and turn it into one of the central forms of the Romantic period, giving it an artistic prestige on the same level as that of opera or symphony. Schubert made writing songs (lieder) into serious art, enabling it to become a respectable vehicle for the most elevated thoughts of the greatest composers.

Schubert wrote more than six hundred songs, as well as nine symphonies, twenty-two piano sonatas, hundreds of short piano pieces, about thirty-five chamber compositions, six Masses, and seventeen operas. Though this output would be astonishing for any composer, it is even more remarkable given Schubert's tragic death in 1828 at the age of thirty-one. A handful of his songs became famous in Vienna during his lifetime, and a few were modestly successful when published privately, selling five or six hundred copies, but nearly all of his large-scale instrumental works were unknown to the general public until a half century after his death. Whatever renown he acquired during his lifetime was as a songwriter, and even this minimal recognition did not extend in any significant way beyond Vienna.

He began composing in earnest in the autumn of 1814 at the age of seventeen while working as an assistant teacher in his father's school. Though he was able to compose only in his spare time, by the end of 1815 he had written almost 150 songs, including his first masterpieces, "Gretchen am Spinnrad" ("Gretchen at the Spinning Wheel") and "Erlkönig" ("The Erl-king"). Both songs were based on texts by Goethe—the first a scene from *Faust*, the second a ballad. Over the course of his brief fifteen-year career, Schubert put music to the words of internationally famous poets, locally known Viennese writers, and friends who were simply part of his inner circle, but it was Goethe who most consistently inspired his greatest work. Sadly, though Schubert wrote more than 70 songs to Goethe's texts, Goethe was unaware of these settings until after Schubert's death. Joseph Spaun, Schubert's devoted friend, sent two volumes of Schubert's songs (including "Erlkönig") to Goethe in the hope that the famous poet would help with publication, but the songs were returned unopened.

"Erlkönig" was probably Schubert's most famous single song during the nineteenth century; however, Goethe's poem was famous long before Schubert set it to music. The poem was originally written in 1782 as part of a ballad opera entitled *Die Fischerin* (The Fisherwoman), and it had already been set to music by several composers within Goethe's inner circle (Johann Reichardt and Carl Zelter being the most prominent) before Schubert was even born. Ballads, particularly those with an element of romantic adventure and the supernatural, were extremely popular in the nineteenth century. (Mary Shelley wrote *Frankenstein* in 1818, three years after Schubert's setting of "Erlkönig.") Goethe based his poem on a Danish ballad,

"*Hr. Oluf han rider,*" derived from old folktales, which had been trans-lated into German by Johann Gottfried von Herder in 1778 as "Erlkönig's Tochter" ("Erl-King's Daughter"). The story, which depicts the death of a child at the hands of the mysterious, super-natural Erl-king, was a perfect vehicle for Schubert, and it beautifully illustrates the eighteen-year-old composer's complete mastery of the dramatic possibilities of this newly emerging art form.

Piano Introduction

When dealing with art song, it is crucial to understand that once a poem is set to music, its meaning is completely transformed. In a song, words no longer have a purely verbal meaning, and music no longer has a purely musical meaning. At every moment, the music means something in the context of the poem that it could not mean by itself, and each word of the poem means something in the con-text of its musical setting that it could not mean by itself. Once music and poetry join forces, it is the combination that is meaningful, and it is the combination that is magical.

EXAMPLE 1

[continued]

EXAMPLE 1 [continued]

In "Erlkönig," this utter inseparability of music and text begins with the first measure of the piece before a single word has even been sung. One of Schubert's brilliant decisions in the song was to make the pounding of the horse's hooves implicit in the poem into a key element of the musical drama and to represent this sound with virtuosic octaves in the pianist's right hand. These repeated octaves are famously difficult to play for even a single measure (try it on your lap!) and utterly exhausting to continue throughout the song as Schubert requires. There is actually a version of the piano part in Schubert's manuscript hand that simplifies this figure from three notes per beat to two, and by Schubert's own admission, this simpler version is the one his limited pianistic technique forced him to play.

EXAMPLE 2

Hearing this simpler version makes it clear that it is the virtuosity and power of the difficult version that instantly creates the dramatic atmosphere of the piece. The repeated octaves in and of themselves are simply a generalized, intense musical gesture. However, when they are combined with the poem—with the image of the pounding horse's hooves and the charged atmosphere of the overall scene—the octaves acquire a specificity and power they could not have on their own. Suddenly, a measure of repeated G's becomes a superb moment of theatrical drama, which in a single gesture sets the mood for the entire song.

The whole fifteen-measure piano introduction (example 1) contains only three brief ideas, and each is set off in bold relief. The octaves that represent the horse's hooves and pound continuously throughout the song are introduced first. They then accompany an ominous bass idea I have labeled "x"—a fast scale up and a slower arpeggio down—and the absence of chords in either hand gives this combination a stark, dramatic power. Both ideas contrast beautifully with the final idea (measures 6 through 8), which has sustained notes, full chords, and a real harmonic progression for the first time in the introduction.

The opening phrase forcefully establishes the G-minor key of the piece, and Schubert immediately begins to repeat the entire opening unit. However, after slightly varying the repeat, he shortens the final measure of the introduction and transposes the ominous bass motive, and this shorter version ("xvar") will recur three times to unify the upcoming stanza. Once again, it is the combination of music and text that is crucial here. On a purely musical level, the transposing and shortening of the bass motive is at best a mildly interesting development. However, this new version's function is as much cinematic as it is musical. It "cuts" from "camera 2"—a general panning of the entire scene in the introduction—to "camera 3," which zooms in on the narrator, who is about to bring us into the dramatic action of the story.

Stanza 1
Narrator

Wer reitet so spät durch Nacht und Wind?
Es ist der Vater mit seinem Kind;
Er hat den Knaben wohl in dem Arm,
Er fasst ihn sicher, er hält ihn warm.

Who rides so late through night and wind?
It is the father with his child;
He holds the boy in the crook of his arm,
He holds him safe, he keeps him warm.

Goethe's poem actually contains four different characters—the narrator, the father, the son, and the Erl-king—and perhaps the most famous aspect of Schubert's setting is the miraculous way he manages to have one singer convey these four distinct personalities. The narrator, in appropriately objective fashion, is the least idiosyncratic in terms of vocal range and musical type. Schubert closely follows Goethe's rigid AABB poetic structure as he sets the scene for us in the opening stanza. The first line of text asks a question, "Wer reitet so spät durch Nacht und Wind?" ("Who rides so late through night and wind?"), and the piano asks a question by repeating the harmonically open-ended "xvar" three times (measures 15 through 20). (Notice how wonderfully the pause in the vocal line in measure 19 gives both the narrator and the listener a moment to peer into the dark to try to see who it is that is riding "so late through night and wind.")

EXAMPLE 3

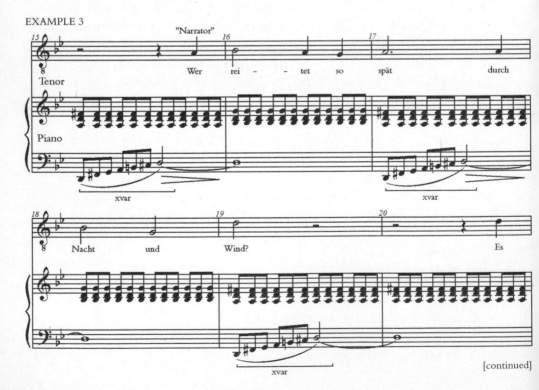

[continued]

EXAMPLE 3 [continued]

ist   der   Va — ter   mit   sei — — — nem

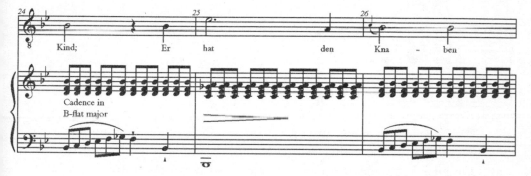

Kind;   Er   hat   den   Kna — ben

Cadence in
B-flat major

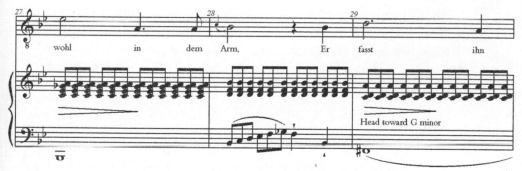

wohl   in   dem   Arm,   Er   fasst   ihn

Head toward G minor

si — cher,   er   hält   ihn   warm.

Return of piano introduction

f

Cadence in G minor

[continued]

EXAMPLE 3 [continued]

The second line of text answers the question, "Es ist der Vater mit seinem Kind" ("It is the father with his child"), and the music punctuates Goethe's half stanza with a clear cadence in B-flat major (measure 24).

The artificial consolation of this major key is short-lived, however, as the final two lines of the stanza—"Er hat den Knaben wohl in dem Arm / Er fasst ihn sicher, er hält ihn warm" ("He holds the boy in the crook of his arm / he holds him safe, he keeps him warm")—bring the music back to G minor and back to the music of the piano introduction.

Stanza 2
Father and Son

„Mein Sohn, was birgst du so bang dein Gesicht?"
„Siehst, Vater, du den Erlkönig nicht?
Den Erlenkönig mit Kron' und Schweif?"
„Mein Sohn, es ist ein Nebelstreif."

"My son, why hide you so anxiously your face?"
"Father, do you not see the Erl-king?
The Erl-king with crown and cloak?"
"My son, it is only a wisp of fog."

Both Goethe and Schubert have set the scene with incredible efficiency and economy in a single opening four-line stanza, and we now plunge immediately into the heart of the drama. Every detail of the music—thematically, harmonically, dynamically, and vocally—is designed to bring the ballad's characters and plot to life. The brief piano interlude after stanza 1, in Beethoven-like fashion, reduces the fifteen-measure piano introduction to its core essence—its first five measures—and the softer, *pianissimo* echo in measure 35 sets the mood for the anxious entry of the father.

Schubert's use of vocal range to characterize the different individuals in the song is extraordinary, and his most powerful dramatic effects are often produced by the simplest means. The father, for example, is immediately defined by his low vocal register. In addition, when he sings *pianissimo* against bare octaves in the piano part, the combination creates an eeric hollowness that perfectly captures his anxiety as he asks, "Mein Sohn, was birgst du so bang dein Gesicht?" ("My son, why hide you so anxiously your face?") As his worry mounts, the vocal line rises up a scale, the music gets louder (with a *crescendo* beginning in measure 38), and the piano part thickens from bare octaves to three- and then four-note chords, followed by the dramatic entry of a real bass line to end the phrase with a clear cadence in measure 40.

EXAMPLE 4

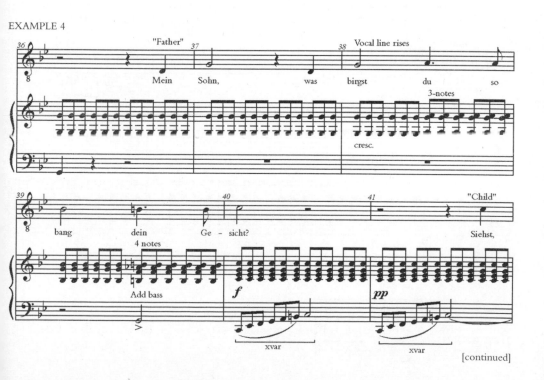

[continued]

EXAMPLE 4 [continued]

If the father is instantly defined by his low vocal range, the son, in contrasting fashion, is defined by his high vocal range as he asks, "Siehst, Vater, du den Erlkönig nicht? Den Erlenkönig mit Kron' und Schweif?" ("Father, do you not see the Erl-king? The Erl-king with crown and cloak?") The father's answer closes the stanza and brings the text to life. First of all, the differences in the vocal ranges of the father and son are clearly marked by having the first note of the father's final line (measure 51) enter a full octave lower than the last note of the son's (measure 50). In addition, the piano's left-hand figure, which has been a unifying element throughout the stanza ("xvar"), now enters on a low F, the lowest note on Schubert's piano, preparing and further emphasizing the "lowness" of the father's voice. Finally, as the father attempts to placate his son—"Mein Sohn, es ist ein Nebelstreif" ("My son, it is only a wisp of fog")—Schubert resolves to a falsely hopeful major key, and this resolution to a complete, major chord on the word *Nebelstreif* (wisp of fog) sounds incredibly reassuring after three measures of hollow octaves in the piano part. Like all great song composers, Schubert is not setting Goethe's words to music as much as he is setting the emotions behind the words.

Stanza 3
Erl-king

„Du liebes Kind, komm, geh mit mir!
Gar schöne Spiele spiel' ich mit dir;
Manch' bunte Blumen sind an dem Strand,
Miene Mutter hat manch gülden Gewand."

"You lovely child, come, go with me.
Many a beautiful game I'll play with you;
Some colorful flowers are on the shore,
My mother has many golden robes."

The entrance of the Erl-king in stanza 3 is one of the great moments in nineteenth-century art song, and once again every element combines to make the drama come to life. Schubert rarely paints death in obviously melodramatic fashion with intense, dissonant chords, in dark minor keys, at loud, fear-inducing volume, but usually chooses instead to represent it as something seductive and alluring, set softly in major keys, with soothing harmony. Everything about the Erl-king's entrance is designed to make him sound appealing to the child, not terrifying, and Schubert's use of harmony, in particular, is wonderfully subtle. Stanza 2, as we have already seen, shifts to a major key (B-flat major) as the father tries to placate his son. The little three-measure piano interlude that follows (measures 55 through 57, example 5) takes this key, gives it a playful, active bass line, and turns it into the Erl-king's key of seduction. The same key now has a completely different meaning and feeling, which prepares us for the Erl-king's entrance and the most striking event in the piece so far (particularly for the tired accompanist!)—stopping the pounding "horses'-hooves" triplets in the piano part.

The halting of these triplets is a brilliant theatrical stroke. Technically speaking, the continuous triplet motion (three notes per beat) continues in the piano part; however, the three notes are now divided between the hands in a far simpler, less aggressive, almost lulling pattern. What this means dramatically is that the horse's hooves are still part of the scene, but the Erl-king's distractions have pushed the galloping into the background. As the eminent critic Donald Tovey puts it, "The galloping is no longer seen; it is felt in [the child's] half sleep."

EXAMPLE 5

[continued]

EXAMPLE 5 [continued]

mir!   Gar schö — — ne Spie — le

Decorate

spiel'_____ ich mit dir;   manch bun — — — te

Blu — men sind__ an   dem Strand,   Mei-ne

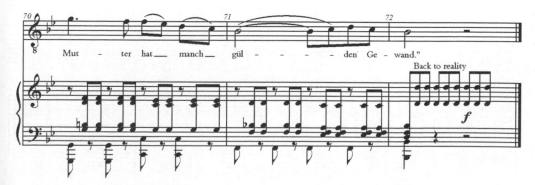

Mut — ter hat__ manch__ gül — — — — den Ge — wand."

Back to reality

f

Everything in this stanza is designed for seduction. The Erl-king whispers *pianissimo* in the child's ear. The key is major. The accompaniment pattern is alluring, not threatening. The harmony is straightforward and all within the key. The Erl-king's melody is lovely and singable, with playful vocal decorations on "spiel'." Death has rarely sounded more enchanting, and the seductive appeal of this stanza is almost physically palpable.

Stanza 4

„Mein Vater, mein vater, und hörest du nicht,
Was Erlenkönig mir leise verspricht?"
„Sei ruhig, bleibe ruhig, mein Kind;
In dürren Blätter säuselt der Wind."

"My father, can't you hear it?
What the Erl-king quietly promises me?"
"Be calm, stay calm my child;
Through dry leaves rustles the wind."

The beginning of stanza 4 is another one of the great moments in Schubert song. The child, on the verge of succumbing to the Erl-king's wiles, forcefully tries to wrench himself free, and the musical translation of this moment could not be more perfect. As the Erl-king cadences, a single note (D) is wrenched out of the chord and once again becomes the pounding horse's hooves dragging us back to reality, away from the Erl-king's fantasy. As the child desperately cries, "Mein Vater, mein Vater," the E-flat of his vocal line grinds in a stunningly dissonant way against the repeated D's in the piano—the perfect musical equivalent of a child's shriek.

EXAMPLE 6

[continued]

EXAMPLE 6 [continued]

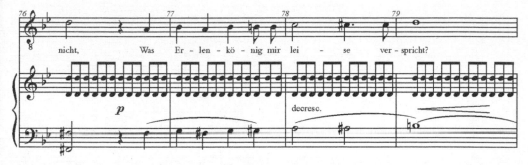

[continued]

EXAMPLE 6 [continued]

Then, in another superb translation of text into music, Schubert represents the father trying to redirect his child's fearful thoughts, by forcefully redirecting his child's music to a remote key (B minor) on the way to another placating cadence in a major key (G major, measure 85). Each of these major-key cadences perfectly captures the father's denial of reality as he continues to pretend, both to himself and to his child, that there is nothing wrong. "It's not the Erl-king; it's nothing but dry leaves rustling in the wind."

Stanzas 5 + 6

„Willst, feiner Knabe, du mit mir gehn?
Meine Töchter sollen dich warten schön;

Meine Töchter führen den nächtlichen Reihn
Und wiegen und tanzen und singen dich ein."

„Mein Vater, mein Vater, und siehst du nicht dort
Erlkonigs Töchter am düstern Ort?"
„Mein Sohn, mein Sohn, ich seh es genau:
Es scheinen die alten Weiden so grau."

"Do you want to come with me, dear boy?
My daughters shall wait on you fine;
My daughters lead the nightly dances
And will rock and dance and sing you to sleep."

"My father, my father, can't you see there
The Erl-king's daughters in the gloomy place?"
"My son, my son, I see it well:
The old willows they shimmer so grey."

During the brief piano interlude between stanzas (measures 85 and 86), Schubert once again turns denial into seduction by subtly transforming the father's "denial-of-reality" key (G major) into the Erl-king's key of seduction (C major). The fantasy that the Erl-king now spins is even more alluring as the galloping triplets in the accompaniment turn into graceful, *pianississimo* arpeggios, and the Erl-king's melody becomes even more attractive and playful. Then, in another simple yet devastatingly effective dramatic stroke, Schubert represents the child's rising terror by bringing back his music from stanza 4 transposed a whole step higher! No instrument is more sensitive to differences of register than the human voice, and hearing the shriek of "Mein Vater, mein Vater" higher is stunningly powerful.

Once again, the father tries to convince both himself and his child that there is nothing to fear, but this time he is unable to do so. He is no longer capable of reaching a cadence in a major key, and the stanza ends instead with a return to the music of the piano introduction, now in the key of D minor.

Stanza 7

„Ich liebe dich, mich reizt deine schöne Gestalt;
Und bist du nicht willig, so brauch' ich Gewalt."
„Mein Vater, mein Vater, jetzt fasst er mich an!
Erlkönig hat mir ein Leids getan!"

"I love you, your beautiful form entices me;
And if you're not willing, I shall use force."
"My father, my father, he's grabbing me now!
The Erl-king has done me harm!"

EXAMPLE 7

[continued]

EXAMPLE 7 [continued]

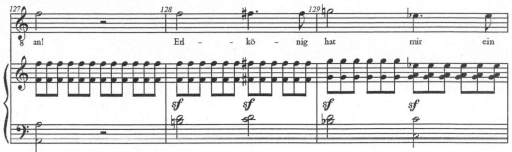

[continued]

EXAMPLE 7 [continued]

The drama reaches its climax in stanza 7, and once again the simplicity of Schubert's most powerful theatrical gestures is remarkable. The Erl-king is about to step out of his disguise and reveal his true nature. To convey this shift of attitude, Schubert shifts keys—from the D minor of the piano interlude to E-flat major for the Erl-king's entrance (measure 116). This key change is as willful and abrupt as the Erl-king's transformation. Games and seductions are over. All is about to be revealed. Covering up the truth with smooth, seamless harmonic connections is no longer necessary. The Erl-king reveals his true desires on "Ich liebe dich, mich reizt deine schöne Gestalt" (I love you, your beautiful form entices me), as he drops his disguise, leaves all major-key fantasies behind, and cadences for the first time in a minor key—"Und bist du nicht willig, so brauch' ich Gewalt" (And if you're not willing, I shall use force).

The piano reacts with horror, at the loudest dynamic in Schubert's universe (*fff*), and in a brilliant theatrical stroke, the music of "Mein Vater, mein Vater" repeats for a third time, now transposed still another half step higher, at the limits of the singer's vocal range—the perfect representation of a child shrieking on the brink of death.

Stanza 8

Dem Vater grauset's; er reitet geschwind,
Er hält in Armen das ächzende Kind,
Erreicht den Hof mit Müh' und Not;
In seinen Armen das Kind war tot.

The father shudders; he rides swiftly,
He holds in his arms the moaning child,
He reaches the farm with effort and need;
In his arms the child was dead.

Great dramatists nearly always save some musical resource to use at key moments, and the final stanza of "Erlkönig" is a perfect example. One of the defining elements of this song has been the virtuosic repeated octaves (horse's hooves) in the right hand of the piano part. These octaves have generated an enormous amount of energy and excitement throughout the piece, and their brief absence during the Erl-king's seductions helped create the song's only moments of relative relaxation. Now, in the final stanza, as the child is being taken by the Erl-king, the opening right-hand octaves return, but for the very first time they are in both hands (measure 131)!

Saving these double-handed octaves for this climactic moment makes for extraordinary theater, but Schubert still has more surprises up his sleeve. Goethe gives the narrator the task of completing the story, and Schubert's simple musical gestures give these final lines incredible dramatic life. To depict the father riding swiftly, Schubert speeds up the music (*accelerando*) while the rising vocal lines add excitement. To convey the father's arrival home, the left hand ascends a chromatic scale—each step more difficult than the last. When the scale/father finally reaches the remote key of A-flat major (example 7, measure 143), the music trails away, getting slower and softer— a perfect representation of the exhausted father collapsing on his doorstep.

Schubert saves his greatest "coup de théâtre" for last. The final line of the song, the dramatic conclusion of the poem—"In seinen Armen das Kind war tot" ("In his arms the child was dead")—is set as musical speech: as recitative. It is the last thing anyone would have expected, and it is a stunning dramatic choice. By playing against the hyperemotionality of the moment, Schubert comes up with the perfect theatrical solution. The tragedy needs no further melodrama, and the factual simplicity of the final, quasi-spoken words—"the child was dead"—followed by the simplest cadence in tonal music ("THE END") is devastating.

"Who Can Do Anything after Beethoven?"

Early in his career, Schubert wrote in his diary, "Secretly in my heart of hearts I still hope to make something of myself, but who can do anything after Beethoven?" Schubert, like nearly every composer in the nineteenth century, was in awe of Beethoven's overwhelming presence. Though there are conflicting accounts as to whether the two ever met, there is no doubt that Beethoven was the dominant imaginative model throughout Schubert's mature artistic life. Schubert was a torchbearer at Beethoven's funeral in 1827, only twenty months before his own, and Schubert's dying wish was to be buried as close to Beethoven as possible.

The literary critic Harold Bloom has a fascinating theory about these kinds of artistic relationships, which he discusses in the book *The Anxiety of Influence*. To vastly oversimplify an enormously sophisticated theory, Bloom starts with the premise that all art is created in response to previous art. A painter paints a tree not in response to seeing a tree but in response to seeing another painting of a tree. The core of Bloom's provocative theory is the idea that weak artists imitate their predecessors, while strong artists creatively misread them. In a creative misreading, an artist takes what he needs from his predecessor—a part of the predecessor's work or technique—and uses it for his own artistic purposes. Poetic history, according to Bloom, is the history of strong poets misreading one another so as to clear imaginative space for themselves.

The applications of this idea not only to Schubert's music but to nearly all nineteenth-century music after Beethoven are profound. In many essential respects, the entire Romantic period can be seen as a series of creative misreadings of Beethoven. Different composers reacted to different aspects of his music in different ways, but almost no one remained outside his influence. In the presence of powerful predecessors, artists tend to either copy those they admire or go in the opposite direction; they rebel in order to define themselves in opposition. A great deal of the most original music of the Romantic era—art songs, tone poems, program symphonies, operas, character pieces, études, and fantasies—clearly results from an attempt to clear imaginative space by working in forms not associated with Beethoven. Schumann, for example, spent more than a decade writing innovative character pieces for the piano, followed by a year of writing songs, before consciously deciding to enter the arena of Beethoven's greatest achievements by writing symphonies and chamber music. Brahms didn't write his first symphony until he was forty-three years old. Schubert, however, like several of the strongest Romantic composers, chose not to shy away from Beethoven's legacy. Though he may have initially found his voice through song, he ultimately neither ran from Beethoven's domain—chamber music, sonata, and symphony—nor copied the master's approach. Instead, he remade these forms in his own image—creatively misread them— appropriating what he needed from Beethoven's compositional technique while redirecting that technique toward his own aesthetic ends. He immersed himself in Beethoven's world, yet emerged intact as Schubert. How the other Romantic composers found a way to clear imaginative space for themselves, find their own voices, and creatively misread Beethoven is the story of the next ten chapters. It is a different story for each composer, yet what they all have in common, consciously or subconsciously, is their joint attempt to answer the central compositional question of the Romantic era—"Who can do anything after Beethoven?"

[8]

Frédéric Chopin
(1810–1849)
A-Minor Mazurka, Op.17, No.4

Chopin has written two wonderful mazurkas which are worth more than forty novels and are more eloquent than the entire century's literature.

—GEORGE SAND

The Romantic Generation

There are certain unique moments in history, what one might call "zeitgeist moments," when an artist or a group of artists can seem to be almost miraculously in sync with the larger society's needs and interests: moments like the Renaissance in Florence, the flowering of opera in Italy, the birth of the Classical style in Vienna, the second Viennese school at the turn of the twentieth century, Paris in the teens and twenties. The art of these moments can seem to grow almost inevitably out of the spirit and circumstances of the time, and the next three chapters focus on one of these moments—the onset of the Romantic period as represented by the three major composers who make up the so-called "Romantic Generation": Chopin, Schumann, and Liszt. Though they were nearly exact contemporaries—Chopin and Schumann were both born in 1810, Liszt in 1811—their music could not have been more different. However, in spite of their differences, the piano was at the heart of their musical sensibilities, and these next three chapters will explore their three strikingly individual approaches to the defining instrument of the nineteenth century.

The piano in its modern incarnation was a relatively new instrument when Chopin, Schumann, and Liszt were born. Though it had been invented at the beginning of the eighteenth century, early versions were more like clavichords than modern pianos, and as late as the 1780s, the harpsichord was still the predominant keyboard instrument in most homes. By 1800, the piano had rendered it obsolete but, as music historian Donald Grout points out, "the piano of the nineteenth century was a quite different instrument from the one for which Mozart had written. Reshaped, enlarged, and mechanically improved, it had been made capable of producing a full, firm tone at any dynamic level, of responding in every way to demands for both expressiveness and overwhelming virtuosity. The piano was the supreme Romantic instrument."

The development and spread of the piano was part of a much larger shift in the fundamental musical culture of the nineteenth-century. For the first time in history, the middle classes were gradually replacing the aristocracy as the principal patrons of music. Publishers and composers began to cater to this large new middle-class public by churning out enormous quantities of easily playable songs, dance music, and pianoforte pieces that could be performed at home or at musical evenings with invited guests. However, in addition to purchasing music for their own use, this same emerging middle-class public was also becoming the audience for the new brand of touring keyboard virtuosos that arose in response to the development and spread of the public concert.

Though today we have become accustomed to thinking of the concert hall as the principal location for music making, during the first half of the nineteenth century, public concerts were the exception rather than the rule, and repertoire exclusively designed for professionals to play and sing for ticket-buying audiences was not nearly as profitable as music designed for domestic music making to be played at home. The new keyboard virtuososi were almost always composers, and they mainly played their own works at benefit concerts (for themselves and other artists) and in private salons. Technical display and novelty was the dominant focus of their performances, and the pianist-composers were tied into an extensive entrepreneurial network involving piano manufacturers, critics, and publishers who symbiotically benefitted from one another's efforts.

It is essential to keep this split between professional and amateur music making in mind if we want to make sense of the full spectrum of nineteenth-century music. To truly understand a particular piece, it is helpful to have a sense of who might have played it, sung it, bought it, or listened to it, as well as a feeling for the setting and context in which it might have been heard. Music written for virtuosos to play before rapt audiences in large concert halls was different from pieces that were more suited to salons or purely private works, and all of these "professional pieces" were completely different from the huge repertoire of piano pieces, sonatinas, duets, songs, and dances designed for amateurs to play and sing at home.

Chopin's Path

Chopin began his compositional career as a typical, if immensely gifted, virtuoso pianist-composer, and the early works he wrote for piano and orchestra, like the *Variations on Là ci darem la mano*, the *Fantasy on Polish Airs*, and the two concertos, were perfect vehicles for the public concerts of the day. However, once he got to Paris in September 1831, he almost completely abandoned concert-hall performances and largely removed himself from the day-to-day dealings of the commercial concert world. He also, surprisingly, made no attempt to write major works in the most prestigious genres of the day—opera, symphony, or chamber music. Instead, he continued to write "pianist's" music, which he played in intimate salons throughout Paris. However, unlike many other composers, who made a clear division between splashy, popular works for public display and serious works for private purposes, Chopin took the forms and gestures of popular salon music and gave them unprecedented artistic substance. He turned salon music into high art, and there is no finer example of this achievement than his lifelong obsession with the mazurka.

From Dancing to Listening: The Mazurka

Chopin's fifty-odd mazurkas were written over the course of his entire mature career, from the early 1830s until his final years. These relatively short pieces, ranging from about thirty seconds to five minutes in length, are some of his greatest compositions, and they provide an intimate window into his artistic soul. The mazurka itself is not a single dance but actually one of a family of Polish folk dances. All of the regional variations have three beats to a measure, and they characteristically accent normally weak beats (accompanied by a tap of the heel)—either the second or third beat of a measure. Other significant features of the dance that appeared to influence Chopin were the fact that it had the character of an improvisation, was sung as often as it was played, was frequently accompanied by a bagpipelike instrument called a *duda*, had a repetitive structure based on two or four parts of six to eight bars each, and in many cases seemed to have no definite ending: either simply repeating until the performers decided to stop, or finishing inconclusively at the end of a measure.

Chopin heard these dances from an early age growing up in Poland, but interestingly enough, there appear to be no direct quotations from any existing songs or dances in his own mazurkas. In fact, the relationship of Chopin's mazurkas to actual Polish folk mazurkas is quite complex. The process of taking a real-world dance and "artifying" it, so to speak, began long before Chopin. A hundred years earlier, Bach's keyboard suites took allemandes, bourées, and sarabandes that were originally meant to be danced to and turned them into sophisticated, abstract music to listen to. Classical-period symphonies, sonatas, and string quartets did the same thing with minuets. In the nineteenth century, however, people became obsessed not just with dance music in general, but with folk music in particular. As cities became more industrial, the idea of folk music from the countryside being somehow purer and more virtuous than art music spread throughout Europe. Folk poetry and folk music became allied with the newly emerging sense of nationalism, and the search for national identity spurred enormous interest in the collection of authentic folk art, folk poetry, and folk music. This newly discovered material was dealt with in many different ways. Some folk music was preserved more or less intact in ethnographic collections. Other material was arranged or transcribed by high-art composers like Beethoven in his arrangements of Scottish songs and Bartók in his *Romanian Dances.* Some composers wrote willfully simple music in imitation folk style—a kind of "faux" folk music. Chopin's mazurkas, however, were neither transcriptions, arrangements, nor imitations of actual folk dances. Instead, Chopin internalized the rhythms, harmonies, melodic figures, gestures, and cadences of the mazurkas he grew up with and combined them with his own musical language in a highly original way. He took what he needed from his source material and invented the rest, creating a uniquely personal synthesis that was as powerfully expressive and emotional as any music he would ever write.

A New Kind of Introduction

Chopin's mazurkas contain some of his most deeply personal and highly original music, and the A–Minor Mazurka from op. 17 is one of Chopin's most remarkable pieces. It is the only mazurka in the op. 17 collection that begins with an introduction, and these four quiet introductory measures are a revolution in microcosm.

EXAMPLE 1

The Classical-period world, with rare exceptions, was a world of unambiguous beginnings and endings. Frames were stable. Keys were clearly defined. The beginning of the A-Minor Mazurka, however, destroys stability and clarity in its very first measure. Though the piece is in the key of A minor, it does not begin on an A-minor chord or even a stable chord, and it does not have a clear cadence in the key of A minor until measure 20! Chopin's conception of what it means to be in a key is radically new. "Home"—the tonic chord—is no longer the place where all musical journeys start and end; it has now become a place we head toward. Chopin's new approach to tonality, incidentally, is not limited to this mazurka. His A-Minor Prelude, for example, is even more radical, as it delays the only A-minor chord in the piece until the final measure. This fluid, dynamic conception of tonality, in which a key is something we head toward rather than reside in, was to have enormous implications as the century progressed.

That the A-Minor Mazurka does not begin on an A-minor chord is unnerving enough, but even more unsettling is the fact that it begins on an ambiguous, dissonant chord, in an uncertain key, and refuses to explain itself. On first hearing, this brief, haunting four-measure introduction seems to be a self-contained fragment, with the piece proper beginning in measure 5; however, if you listen closely, there is actually a beautiful and subtle connection between the two sections. Hidden in the middle of the opening three chords is a tiny, whispered three-note fragment of melody—B–C–D. Chopin repeats the three notes—B–C–D—then starts to repeat them a third time (B, C . . .), but this time decorates the D—D–E–D—which "resolves" ambiguously (up or down?) to end the introduction with a question mark.

What was the point of these four measures? They seem to begin in mid-thought and end without resolution, creating a deeply expressive atmosphere of longing and regret in a single, four-measure gesture. Though there seems to be no connection between this introduction and the tune that begins the main body of the mazurka in measure 5, if you listen closely, the first three notes of the mazurka tune are the same three notes—B, C, D—that the introduction has subtly and painstakingly prepared! The melody seems to emerge as if from a trance, beginning with the introduction's little dream-fragment B, C, D and then taking flight. The harmonic and thematic ambiguity of this introduction and its dreamlike foreshadowing of the main mazurka theme are what Romanticism is all about. Instead of initial clarity,

Chopin, like so many Romantic composers, prefers a gradually unfolding illumination of meaning, and we will not grasp the full significance of these opening four measures until the mazurka's final phrase.

The Core Idea

The first eight measures of this exquisite melody are almost a primer on what makes Chopin great. Because they are the key to the entire mazurka and contain in capsule form so much that is characteristic of Chopin's approach to melody, decoration, rhythm, harmony, and tonality, I want to look extremely closely at how they work, parameter by parameter, before putting the elements back together to see how the phrase works as a whole. Let's start with rhythm.

Though the rhythm of the melody throughout this mazurka often sounds as if it is being improvised, it is actually carefully and subtly controlled. I have written two different versions of measures 5 through 8 with more predictable, less-interesting rhythm. My first version eliminates all of Chopin's dotted rhythms (long-short) and replaces them with even notes, creating a bland, undifferentiated melody with no individual character or dancelike energy.

EXAMPLE 2A

EXAMPLE 2B

My second version goes in the opposite direction, adding dotted rhythms everywhere, creating a nervous, jumpy, utterly inelegant phrase. Keeping these two versions in mind helps point out the beauties of Chopin's version. His opening dotted rhythm immediately gives the melody a dancelike energy. The impulsive little grace note in measure 6 (example 1) creates a feeling of spontaneous improvisation, followed by even notes that push the line forward as the opening three-note scale (B–C–D) now flowers upward to become a "huge" six-note scale. A final dotted rhythm in measure 7 creates a beautiful hesitation that slows down the music's forward momentum and marks the melody's halfway point (measure 8).

The rhythmic activity of these first four bars slows down in the second four bars, and once again rhythmic subtlety is the difference between good and great. I have written a bland version of these next four measures that simply repeats the rhythm of measure 9 four times.

EXAMPLE 3

My square version immediately points out the character and energy created by Chopin's surprising short-long rhythm on the downbeats of measures 11 and 12 (example 1). However, it is not only the rhythm of the melody that is subtly controlled but its shape as well. Though the contour of the melody sounds almost improvised, if you remove Chopin's decorations and keep only the first note of each measure, you can immediately see how the melody rises up a simple scale in the first half of the phrase (B–C–D–E–F#) then down in the second half (F#–F♮–E).

EXAMPLE 4

It is the clarity of this underlying structure that allows Chopin to decorate the melody so freely, and the remarkable harmonic freedom of this phrase is a result of an equally clear structure. We have already seen that Chopin keeps the sense of key ambiguous by avoiding any A-minor chords in this opening, and this continues when the melody begins in measure 5 with a D-minor chord. Measures 6 and 7 start to head toward a major key (C major); however, instead of resolving as expected, Chopin turns poignantly—hopes of a major key dashed—to an E-minor chord.

EXAMPLE 5A

Kapilow "normal" resolution

EXAMPLE 5B

Chopin resolution

At this point we have no idea where the phrase is heading, and in a way that almost anticipates Debussy, Chopin basically slides a single *dominant-seventh chord** down the scale three times, with each finger moving to the next nearest note on the keyboard, like this:

EXAMPLE 6

Kapilow reduction

However, Chopin poignantly decorates this simple progression.

EXAMPLE 7

As the passage ends, we suddenly find ourselves on the verge of a cadence in A minor, the home key, but instead of resolving, the second phrase begins a varied repeat of the first phrase, and once again, no A-minor chord is anywhere to be found.

What is important to understand in the midst of all of this detail is the key forward-backward nature of the phrase. Like the opening of the *Waldstein* Sonata, going forward, the music sounds utterly confusing, as if Chopin is shifting keys nearly every measure. He begins ambiguously, in no clear key, and then seems to head toward C major. However, that cadence is thwarted, leaving the harmonic situation even more confused. Then a free-fall slide down a scale surprisingly washes out on the verge of the home key, but that cadence is also unresolved. The music sounds as if it is wandering almost randomly from key to key, but if you follow the bass line (the lowest voice in the left hand), it is actually tracing out the identical pattern we saw in the opening of the *Waldstein* Sonata: a stepwise descent from tonic to dominant. From A to E–**A**–G–F♯–F♮–**E**. The music has really been "in A minor" (under its control) all along, though in a completely new way. What sounds confusing going forward makes perfect sense looking backward. What sounds spontaneous and improvisatory is actually superbly logical and structured. To use E. M. Forster's phrase again, the phrase is "surprising in convincing ways."

The Art of Decoration

The reason I have described these eight measures in such detail is not only because they contain so much material that is quintessentially Chopinesque, but because Chopin courageously stakes nearly the entire fate of this mazurka on the beauty of this single phrase. Of the sixty measures that make up the A section of this ABA piece, forty-seven are varied repeats of this one phrase! Aside from the four-measure introduction and a single, contrasting, eight-measure idea, the entire A section of this mazurka is "about" this opening phrase.

The almost obsessive repetition at the heart of this mazurka is part of the nature of the folk dance itself, but Chopin's approach to repetition in this piece is extraordinarily sophisticated. The second phrase of the mazurka proper (measures 13 through 20) is clearly a varied repeat of the first phrase with elaborate decorations that sound as if they are being improvised on the spot. Chopin adored opera, and one of his great compositional achievements was to create a kind of instrumental equivalent to the ornate vocal decorations found in bel canto opera. Though these decorations might sound as if they are being improvised by the performer, they are actually carefully controlled by Chopin.

Measure 13 decorates each melody note of measure 5 (see asterisks on score in example 1) with the note above it or below it, weaving a beautiful arabesque of nine notes from the original four. To make sure the listener knows her place in the phrase, the next measure (measure 14) copies the original exactly to lead directly to measure 15—the measure that is the heart and soul of this mazurka. Nothing in the restrained decorations of measure 13 or measure 14 prepares us in any way for the extravagant, spellbinding, fifteen-note decoration of measure 15. This is the kind of moment Chopin's exquisitely sensitive pianism thrived on. According to all contemporary accounts, Chopin's piano sound wasn't loud or brilliant enough for large concert halls, but when he was in an intimate salon, surrounded by a small circle of kindred spirits, the emotional impact of his playing was overwhelming. His delicacy of touch, dynamic shading, and flexibility of rhythm were the envy of the greatest pianists of the day, and extraordinary measures like this one (as well as the even more beautiful variation in measure 31) give us a good sense of what his playing must have been like.

The other variations in this phrase are less ornate, but each one registers. Compare, for example, measure 17, with its wonderful rest on the downbeat, with measure 9. Any other composer would have simply repeated this pattern lower in measure 18 (see example 8A). Instead, Chopin's unexpected, quick six-note decoration is heart-stopping (see example 8B), and before we have a chance to recover, a sudden leap to the highest note of the entire section leads to the long-awaited cadence in A minor that completes the opening unit. (Notice how the octaves in the left hand in measure 19—the only octaves in the section—prepare this key cadence.)

EXAMPLE 8A   EXAMPLE 8B

Kapilow normal continuation   Chopin   Highest note   Cadence in A min.

The One Other Idea

This one sixteen-measure phrase (measures 5 through 20) is the core of the piece. As in a folk mazurka, the entire sixteen-measure idea is immediately repeated; however, Chopin adds just enough exquisite variation (three of the sixteen measures) to keep his listeners on the edges of their seats, yearning for each new, sigh-inducing ornament. The one other idea in this A section lasts for only eight measures, and it too is all about subtle decorations. At heart, the phrase simply

repeats and varies a sinuous, two-measure melody over a *pedal point**
in the bass.

EXAMPLE 9

What gives life to the phrase are the small changes in each repeat.
None of the two-measure pairs are exactly alike, and the subtle variations in rhythm, melody, and harmony keep the listener waiting to
hear what comes next. The phrase, however, lasts for only eight measures before it leads back to our opening tune. One final repeat ends
the section with a magical resolution to A major, not A minor, and
the incredible shift of mood created by this beautiful major-key
cadence ushers in the trio, or middle section, of the movement.

EXAMPLE 10

[continued]

EXAMPLE 10 [continued]

Trio

Trios in dance forms, as we saw in Haydn's minuet, traditionally function as moments of relaxation, and this trio is no exception. After the extraordinary harmonic and melodic complexity of the A section, the trio's bright major key, simple harmony, and straightforward melody come as an enormous relief. I mentioned earlier that many folk mazurkas were accompanied by a bagpipelike instrument called a *duda*, and an imitation-bagpipe drone in the left hand dominates this trio, repeating the notes A and E on eighty-six of the section's ninety beats.

The melody is as straightforward as the harmony. A four-measure descending duet is balanced by four ascending measures, and the

EXAMPLE 11

[continued]

EXAMPLE 11 [continued]

whole eight-measure phrase is repeated with slight variation. Then, in utterly symmetrical fashion, Chopin repeats all sixteen measures but alters the final two bars (measures 91 and 92) to shift back to minor and lead to the return of the A section.

Coda

As is typical in these mazurkas, the return of the A section is shortened, and after two phrases, Chopin adds a twenty-four-measure coda. Beginning with op. 17, Chopin begins to add increasingly expansive, highly original codas to his mazurkas, and the coda to the A-Minor Mazurka is remarkable in many ways.

EXAMPLE 12

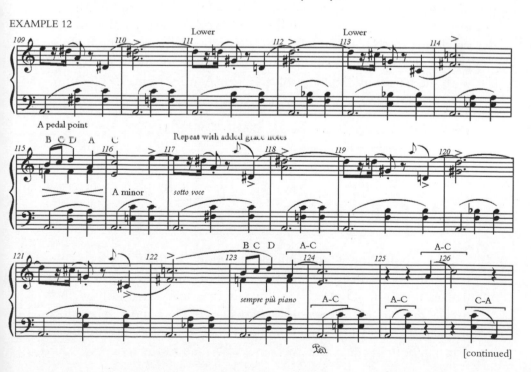

[continued]

EXAMPLE 12 [continued]

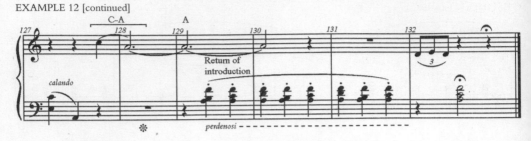

First, there is a balance between stability and dissonance that is quin-tessentially Chopinesque. On the one hand, this coda could not be more harmonically grounded, as it has an A pedal point (the tonic note) in every measure. However, the angular melody and the harmony above the pedal point are startlingly dissonant. They both essentially slide down chromatically, producing a series of highly dissonant, unresolved chords that finally wash out at an A-minor cadence in measures 115 and 116. After all of the dissonance in the phrase, the clear cadence and smoother melodic line come as a relief and begin to provide closure to the piece.

The whole phrase then repeats sotto voce (literally, "under the voice"—in a subdued manner) while the addition of a grace-note leap every two measures creates a wonderfully exotic keyboard sonority. However, when we come to the cadence a second time at measures 123 and 124, we suddenly realize with a shock that this lit-tle closing melody—B–C–D–A–C—is actually the opening melodic gesture of the entire mazurka. It is the melody of measures 5 and 6 with the harmony finally resolved to an A-minor chord! The unre-solved, original version finally resolves in the home key.

EXAMPLE 13A   EXAMPLE 13B

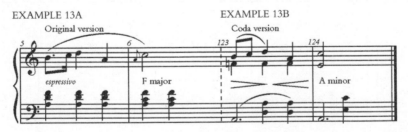

At this point, the work of the piece is done, but Chopin feels com-pelled to go further. The opening five-note melodic gesture of the mazurka is B–C–D–A–C. Chopin, in Beethoven-like fashion, now focuses on just the final two notes of the gesture—A and C. He reduces the whole piece to this single interval, then turns the interval upside down in both hands as A–C becomes C–A, and finally reduces C–A to just A. The technique of reducing an entire piece to a single note comes directly from Beethoven; however, for Beethoven, these kinds of reductions are answers; for Chopin, they are questions. Even when we are reduced to our core essence, for Chopin we are still a mystery. As the A of C–A holds (measure 129), the introduction floats in as a beautiful bookend to close the piece in classic mazurka fashion—without resolution and with nostalgic yearning. The piece begins in mid-thought and ends in midair. The piece is finished yet poetically incomplete.

The Privilege of a Lifetime

Chopin's career was as original and unique as his music. At a time when being a famous composer meant writing huge symphonies and operas, Chopin declined to participate. In a career of amazing focus and integrity, Chopin included the piano in every piece he composed. Though he adored opera more than any other kind of music, as far as we know he never even began a sketch. Chopin knew who he was, and, equally important, who he was not. He played the piano with his own unique sound and with his own unique physical approach. When he realized that he had neither the temperament nor the extroversion necessary for a public virtuoso career, he simply stopped performing in public. He wrote the music he wanted to write, for the instrument he loved. Nothing less, nothing more.

Chopin, perhaps more than any other composer I know of, epitomizes the Joseph Campbell quotation I mentioned in chapter 1: "The privilege of a lifetime is being who you are." Being who he was, was all Chopin cared to be, because he knew that it was his only choice. He had the courage to believe that the expression contained in a forty-second piano prelude or a four-minute mazurka was as powerful and as important as the expression contained in a huge four-hour Wagner opera. And though the body of work he left us in his brief thirty-nine years is small in scope when compared to the oeuvre of Mozart or Bach, because it completely represents one individual's inner world, it is powerful and complete. Chopin's creativity may have begun and ended at the keyboard of a piano, but what he heard there was so profoundly original and powerful that more than 150 years after his death we are still listening to try to grasp all that he heard.

[9]

Robert Schumann
(1810–1856)

"Träumerei" from *Kinderszenen*

The painter turns a poem into a painting; the musician sets a picture to music.

—ROBERT SCHUMANN

The Romantic Fragment

When we think about the Romantic period, what often springs to mind is music that makes a massive public statement, like the colossal operas of Wagner, the monumental symphonies and tone poems of Berlioz, Richard Strauss, and Mahler, and the extravagant virtuoso works of Liszt and Paganini. However, the nineteenth century made equally important musical contributions at the other end of the compositional spectrum with the intimate, private, lyrical expression of art song and the piano miniature, and it was in this arena that Schumann first made his mark. Up until 1840, all of Schumann's published music was written for the piano. *Papillons*, *Carnaval*, the *Davidsbündlertänze*, *Kreisleriana*, and *Kinderszenen* were all composed during these years, and these pieces contain some of the most original music written in the nineteenth century. Sets of character pieces grouped into loosely organized cycles like these became a model for other composers of the period, and the genre's popularity extended not only throughout the nineteenth century but well into the twentieth century as well.

The power of Schumann's collections comes from his mastery of what Charles Rosen has called the Romantic Fragment. A Romantic Fragment is an individual piece that is complete in and of itself but, like an individual song in a song cycle, depends on the other pieces in the collection for its full meaning. Paradoxically, a Romantic Fragment is both complete and incomplete. It exists as a self-contained piece in the present, but requires a past and a future to complete its expression. Some fragments are literally incomplete. The first song of Schumann's cycle *Dichterliebe*, for example, ends on a dissonant chord, which resolves only at the beginning of the cycle's second song. However, even when a fragment is not literally incomplete, to use Rosen's words, it "projects beyond itself in a provocative way." Its resonance is open, not closed, and this tension between something that is both complete and incomplete is at the heart of the fragment and at the heart of one of Schumann's most famous pieces—"Träumerei" ("Dreaming") from *Kinderszenen* (*Scenes from Childhood*).

"Seemingly, but Only Seemingly, Simple"

In 1838 Schumann wrote to Clara Wieck, the great concert pianist who was to become his wife, "I've put on my frilly dress and composed 30 cute little things from which I've selected about 12 and called them '*Scenes from Childhood*.' They are like an echo to what you once wrote to me, that I sometimes 'seem like a child' to you." Aaron Copland once described the style of Martha Graham, his choreographer for *Appalachian Spring*, as "seemingly, but only seemingly, simple," and the thirteen pieces that make up Schumann's *Kinderszenen* are also only seemingly simple.

EXAMPLE 1

[continued]

EXAMPLE 1 [continued]

"Träumerei" is the seventh piece in *Kinderszenen*, and its very first note is a testament to the way a Romantic Fragment's meaning can be subtly affected by the pieces surrounding it in a collection. The piece that precedes "Träumerei," "Wichtige Begebenheit" ("An Important Event"), ends with a strong, energetic cadence in the key of A major.

EXAMPLE 2

"Träumerei" begins with a single note—a C. With the final A-major chord of "Wichtige Begebenheit" still in our ears, we hear this C as a shift in key from A major to A minor. However, when the C is followed by an F and an F-major chord, we suddenly discover that we have subtly shifted keys to F major on "Träumerei"'s opening note. The C has one meaning going forward from the previous piece, but a different meaning after the second note of "Träumerei" has been heard. If "Träumerei" is played as an independent piece (as an encore, for example), the piece simply begins in F major. There is no tonal ambiguity, no blurred edge, no mystery, and no "dream." The subtle nuance of the Romantic Fragment is replaced by the far less interesting stability and clarity of an independent piano miniature.

The beautiful tonal ambiguity of "Träumerei"'s opening is enhanced by an equally subtle rhythmic ambiguity. The piece begins with three-and-a-half beats of "settling-in" music as the melody waits for the chord underneath to establish itself in our ear. (The upbeat and downbeat are labeled "And 1" on the music.) The melody then rises in a graceful, five-note arpeggio to an F (remember this F for later) and repeats the note with a beautiful held chord underneath to finish the gesture. (Note the lovely, quick grace notes in the left hand that emphasize this arrival.) In a subtle way, the rhythm of this opening gesture "dreams." A normal version with clear, square rhythm would shorten the "settling-in" process by one beat so that the second chord could arrive firmly on a downbeat, like this:

EXAMPLE 3

But Schumann's second melody note "dreams" for an extra beat, causing the second chord to arrive poetically in the middle of measure 2, not on a downbeat. Once Schumann's arpeggio reaches its top note, the rest of the idea beautifully balances this ascent by gracefully winding its way back down the same distance, F–F, via a decorated scale—F, E, D, C, B♭, A, G—with the resolution back to F coinciding elegantly with the return of the opening idea in measure 5. This exquisitely balanced melodic phrase does not contain a single *accidental** (note outside the key) in its first four measures. The F–F, F-major universe of the piece could not be more clearly or elegantly defined.

In fact, it is this very clarity that makes the second half of the phrase (measures 5 through 8) so striking. Measure 5 begins by repeating the opening "settling-in" gesture and the graceful five-note arpeggio. But this time, the arpeggio arches up higher, to an A instead of an F, and the "dissonant" chord underneath the A, which contains the first accidental in the piece, strikingly emphasizes this new top note. This one moment changes the entire composition. Suddenly, dissonance—minor chords, *diminished chords,** and accidentals—becomes part of the vocabulary of the piece, and the higher arpeggio alters the melody's course as the phrase continues.

Form: Broadway vs. Schumann

The overall AABA form of this piece could not be clearer. Measures 1 through 8 are the opening A section of the piece. The double dots at the end of measure 8 are a sign to repeat the whole section. Measures 9 through 16 are the contrasting, eight-bar B section, and measures 17 through 24 make up the closing, eight-measure A section. "Träumerei" is an absolutely perfect thirty-two-bar song form:

A (eight measures), A (eight measures), B (eight measures), A (eight measures). Interestingly enough, this thirty-two-bar form is also the form of nearly every Broadway theater song from Gershwin to Sondheim; however, Schumann uses the form for completely different aesthetic purposes. In a popular song, everything is dependent on the opening idea. As Richard Rodgers said, "If the song is successful, it's the idea that you walk out whistling." On the most basic level, in a theater song, all of the repetitions of the opening idea are designed to imprint it in the listener's ear so that it will be easily remembered and "easily whistled." In "Träumerei," however, the point of repeating and remembering the opening idea is to appreciate the way it is developed and varied as the piece moves forward.

In a theater song, the B section functions primarily as contrast: a move "away" from A that generates a desire to hear it again. Schumann's B section does provide contrast, but that is only part of its purpose. It starts with the "settling in" music and the graceful ascending arpeggio that bridges measures 1 and 2, as if to begin a third repeat of the A section. We have already heard this arpeggio ascend to an F and to an A, and the repeat has cemented these two different versions in our ear. The B section now introduces yet a *third* version, which this time ascends to an E-flat (measure 10) followed by a *fourth* version (after a graceful descent), which repeats the third version higher (measures 13 through 16) to finish the B section. This kind of complex, rich development is a far cry from the "B-section-as-contrast" of a typical theater song. Schumann is interested not simply in creating contrast, but also in enriching our understanding of the piece's opening idea.

It is not only the melody that is developing, but the harmony as well. Schumann changes keys twice; first to G minor in measure 11, then to B-flat major in measure 13. Then, on the verge of a full cadence in yet a third key (D minor in measure 16), at the last instant, with a *ritardando* (an indication to slow down) marked so the listener will not miss the moment, Schumann shifts direction and magically arrives back "home" in F major to begin the final A section.

Saving the Best for Last

By now, the listener has already had to process an enormous amount of sophisticated musical information in a short space of time, but

Schumann has saved the best for last. The return of A begins without surprise as the first four measures of the piece are repeated exactly in measures 17 through 20. Then, in a moment that almost defines Schumann, the entire climax of the piece turns on a single, exquisitely subtle *reharmonization*.* We come to our graceful, ascending arpeggio for the final time. We have already heard four versions of this arpeggio. The melody now floats up to an A exactly as it did in measure 6, but Schumann completely changes the harmony underneath, discovering a miraculous, otherworldly chord that transforms the color of this A. (Schumann writes a *fermata** to make sure we luxuriate in this incredibly beautiful chord.) This kind of exquisite, lyrical moment is what Schumann is all about. Yet what makes this moment so beautiful is, of course, everything that has preceded it—all the other versions of this seemingly simple arpeggio.

Then, as if that were not enough, he rewrites the rest of the phrase so that it ends with a superb final cadence that is also "seemingly, but only seemingly, simple." Measure 23 begins as a copy of measure 3. Then, in yet another exquisite reharmonization (with the apostrophes clearly showing his musical intent), Schumann takes the four-note melody that began the measure—G, A, B♭, D—and repeats it with new, poignant, dark minor-key chords underneath. Like a cloud suddenly darkening the sun, a shadow comes over the music, and the effect is made even more striking by the slowing down of the tempo over the whole phrase. Then, in a wonderful final cadence, Schumann takes the first three notes of this melody—G, A, B♭—and copies them lower as D, E, F to end the piece. This kind of poetical connection is utterly unlike anything by Beethoven. It is as if a melodic snippet—G, A, B♭, D—suddenly caught Schumann's fancy and spontaneously suggested new chords underneath and then the perfect ending. A little three-note fragment that has been a hidden presence throughout the piece becomes a final gesture that is somehow both completely surprising and inevitable at the same time. And even though the piece has ended with a conclusive final cadence, like a true Romantic Fragment its resonance is open, as the work's first melodic gesture (C–F) and "settling-in" music poetically generate the opening of the piece that follows—"Am Kamin" ("At the Fireside").

EXAMPLE 4

The Past That Never Was

During his lifetime, Schumann was probably more famous as a critic and a writer about music than he was as a composer. His father was a bookseller, and his early life was filled with words. He was completely caught up in the world of Romantic literature and poetry, and the German Romantic writer Jean Paul was his literary idol. He wrote and read poetry obsessively, and he was perhaps the most erudite and educated of the Romantic composers. He learned Latin at age seven, and French and Greek at age eight, and his love affair with language and literature was reflected in music that was intensely poetic and imagistic. While the most superficial forms of nineteenth-century program music attempted to literally tell a story in music, Schumann's approach to the genre was far subtler. Rather than attempting to replicate a narrative, Schumann took a subject, a personality, or an image as a starting point or a suggestion for a piece of music that ultimately absorbed and transcended that subject in the composition. The music was in no way "equivalent" to its source ("Träumerei" was not a depiction of an actual dream), but instead took something that might be hinted at in words and expressed it through music's uniquely abstract vocabulary. When the critic Ludwig Rellstab tried to literalize the relationship between Schumann's music and its source in *Kinderszenen* by calling the pieces "snapshots of child life," Schumann replied,

> Anything more inept and narrow-minded I have never come across, than what Rellstab has written about my *Kinderszenen*. He really thinks that I place a crying child before me and then search for tones accordingly. It is the other way around. However I do not deny that while composing, some children's heads were hovering around me, but of course the titles originated afterwards and are, indeed, nothing but delicate directions for execution and interpretation.

Schumann believed that music and poetry sprang from the same source, and this is crucial to remember if we wish to avoid a frequent misunderstanding of the program music of Schumann and other nineteenth-century composers. Because the titles and programs of many Romantic pieces like *Kinderszenen* were clearly written after the music and often as a response to the music, modern critics and audiences tend to dismiss their importance as if these labels were merely ex-post-facto "justifications" or "rationalizations" of already written, absolute music. However, for the Romantics the intimate relationship between literature and music went in both directions. A work of literature or a poetic image might generate a musical response; however, the reverse was equally possible: a piece of music might call up a literary or poetic response. This belief that words and ideas might be both an inspiration and a reaction to music is at the heart of a great deal of the flowery, image-laden music criticism of the period. The subjective response of the individual was everything, whether that individual was a composer, a listener, or a critic. As Schumann put it so succinctly, "I do not take things objectively the way things really are, but rather the way I perceive them subjectively within myself."

It is this elevating of subjective perception above all else that is ultimately the key to understanding the music of *Kinderszenen*. The childhood that *Kinderszenen* "depicts" existed only in Schumann's mind. His own early life was filled with turmoil. During Schumann's infancy, Napoleon's army went through Schumann's hometown twice—once on the way to Russia and then back in desperate defeat, causing complete havoc and consternation. When Schumann's mother developed typhus, he was sent away to live with a surrogate mother. His sister committed suicide when he was fifteen, and his father died ten months later. Both of his parents were of questionable psychological stability, as was Schumann himself. The music of *Kinderszenen* is not about Schumann's actual childhood—"the way things really were"—but rather about his subjective perception of a memory, or perhaps more accurately of a wish.

The wish for a perfect childhood like the one depicted in Schumann's music is, of course, part of all of us, and the poignancy and power of this wish is perhaps directly related to the impossibility of its attainment. The childhood world of *Kinderszenen* may have existed only in Schumann's imagination, yet this world is no less real for its being imaginary. We are our wishes and fantasies as much as we are our realities. And no matter what the facts might have been for Schumann, under *Kinderszenen*'s spell we can have, as his titles suggest, an experience of the most sublimely enchanting childhood one could ever imagine—a world of "foreign lands and peoples," "curious stories," "important events," "perfect happiness," "fears," and finally "peaceful slumber" and "dreams." This vision of childhood may be only a wish and a dream, but as Shakespeare and Freud remind us, we should take our dreams seriously. In the end, we *are* the stuff that dreams are made of.

[10]

Franz Liszt
(1811–1886)
Transcendental Étude in A Minor

Le concert, c'est moi.

—FRANZ LISZT

"The Paganini of the Piano"

By all contemporary accounts, Liszt was the greatest pianist of the
nineteenth century, and he had an enormous impact on Romantic-
period music as both a performer and a composer. Liszt was in many
ways the nineteenth century's equivalent of today's rock stars, and his
public performances generated a kind of adulation and hysteria that
was unprecedented in the history of classical music. The solo piano
recital, for all intents and purposes, owes its existence to Liszt. During the first quarter of the nineteenth century, nearly all public
concerts featured mixed programs of both instrumental and vocal
music. Variety was the key to successful programming, and a typical
concert might include ten or fifteen pieces, ranging from orchestral
overtures to Italian opera selections, trios, concertos, songs, and symphonies. In 1811, the year Liszt was born, the Parisian critic J. L.
Geoffroy wrote, "A public concert is not the place for a piano. . . . This

instrument, made for accompanying, runs a great risk when it is played by itself." It wasn't until the 1830s that programs of purely solo music began to come into existence, and the first use of the term "recital" occurred in conjunction with Liszt's solo performances in London in June 1840. As Therese Ellsworth points out in *The Piano in Nineteenth-Century British Culture,* "Because the word was commonly used to denote the recitation by heart of a poem or a story, advertisements for Liszt's concerts stated that he would offer 'recitals' of his recent fantasies, meaning the performance or the 'reading'—from memory—of each piece."

Everything about these new solo performances or recitals was designed to enhance their theatricality. Liszt was the first pianist to turn the piano sideways so that the audience would be able to see his hands fly across the keyboard. Playing by memory also became essential in order to create the illusion that the pianist, like an opera singer, was not simply performing a piece of music but reciting a dramatic narrative. Performance became theater, women swooned, and Liszt reveled in his role as the nineteenth century's greatest musical showman.

Liszt began his performing career at the age of eleven, and from 1823 to 1848, when he retired from concert life, he dazzled Europe with his astounding keyboard virtuosity. There were two defining experiences that shaped his musical personality. The first was the eighteen months he spent at the age of twelve studying piano with his mentor, Carl Czerny, to whom he ultimately dedicated the *Transcendental* Études. It was Czerny's rigorous, systematic, technical training that laid the foundation for Liszt's "transcendental" piano technique, but it was Paganini who gave Liszt a purpose and a vision for that technique.

When Liszt first heard Paganini play in Paris in April 1832, it was a life-altering experience. It wasn't just Paganini's astounding virtuosity that stupefied him; it was the way Paganini penetrated to the very core of the instrument's personality. As Liszt's biographer Alan Walker puts it, "Henceforth [Liszt] would make it his aim to play the piano not only better than anyone else, but to play it as well as it can be played—a very different proposition. He would become the Paganini of the piano."

But how to transfer to the keyboard what Paganini was doing on the violin? Liszt tried to work this out by writing two groups of studies under Paganini's influence in the 1830s—the six *Paganini Studies* and the *Transcendental* Études. Both pieces went through several versions. The first version of the *Transcendental* Études was composed when Liszt was thirteen and published when he was fifteen years old, before he had ever heard Paganini. These twelve "exercises," as he called them at the time, are completely uninteresting musically, and they are not even difficult to play. They are studies, not concert pieces. Eleven years later, in 1837, Liszt published *Twelve Great Studies for the Piano*, eleven of which are rewritings of his earlier exercises. However, the 1837 revisions are so extensive that the original versions are almost unrecognizable. The *Twelve Great Studies* are probably as difficult to play as anything ever written for the piano, and Liszt only slightly simplified them in his final 1851 version, which is the version nearly always performed today.

As pianist/scholar Charles Rosen points out, however, what is most striking about the brilliant second and third versions of these études is the fact that their basic melodic lines, harmonies, and rhythms are often identical to the mediocre original versions. Liszt kept the essential musical materials intact but completely transformed the pianistic surface and the sound of the music in a way that turned an unoriginal set of student exercises into a virtuosic masterpiece. To get a feeling for how Liszt created this new world of pianistic possibilities, let's look closely at the various stages of development of several core passages in the A-Minor *Transcendental* Étude.

In the Beginning

The first version of the piece, composed when Liszt was thirteen, began like this:

EXAMPLE 1

[continued]

EXAMPLE 1 [continued]

Earlier, I quoted Stravinsky as saying that all creativity begins with observation—with noticing—and it is extraordinary what Liszt notices in this opening. Simple though the music is, if you are paying attention to anything in this excerpt, it is probably the melody in the right hand. But what Liszt notices is the insignificant, repeated note in the thumb of the left hand.

EXAMPLE 2

Even in the context of the left hand alone, you barely notice it.

EXAMPLE 3

But those repeated E's in the thumb become the key to a brand-new, fantastic introduction to the piece in Liszt's later version.

EXAMPLE 4

Since this transformation is quintessential Liszt, let's look step-by-step to see how it is accomplished. Here are the original repeated E's:

EXAMPLE 5

The later version begins by playing them once an octave higher, and then adds a second note—a dissonant note—when the idea repeats.

EXAMPLE 6

Once Liszt has created this new combination, he alternates it with two notes in the left hand to make yet another combination.

EXAMPLE 7

He then creates a final, fantastic cross-handed pattern out of the original, insignificant E's by running the E's together with different notes
above, in alternation with left-hand notes.

EXAMPLE 8

What happens to the tune of the original version is even more
remarkable. Liszt keeps all of its essential elements intact, while completely transforming the surface of the music. The opening four
measures of the tune originally went like this:

EXAMPLE 9

This was the virtuoso second version of 1837:

EXAMPLE 10

Here is the slightly simplified final version of 1851:

EXAMPLE 11

Since once again this is core Liszt technique, let's see how it's done. The essential melody of all three versions begins in the right hand like this:

EXAMPLE 12

The second version keeps all the same notes in the left hand, but puts the repeated E's an octave higher, separating out the two parts clearly, while creating a huge, virtuoso stretch for the left hand as the scale gets lower and lower. At the same time, the right hand turns the simple original melody into an astonishingly difficult one. This version is so difficult to play at tempo that Liszt simplified it in the final version to octaves in the right hand. What is important to understand here is that the essential musical content of all three versions in terms of melody, harmony, and rhythm is identical. However, by utilizing the possibilities of the modern piano to transform the surface of the music, Liszt has turned his uninteresting student exercise into an amazing virtuoso showpiece.

The one other main tune in this étude is also a superb example of Liszt's stunningly original pianistic imagination. Here is the opening of the original version:

EXAMPLE 13

[continued]

EXAMPLE 13 [continued]

The third version takes the single-line right hand of the original version and adds a second note on each beat (notice Liszt's indication to "roll" the two notes so the audience will not miss the extra note), making it much more difficult to play and more interesting to listen to.

EXAMPLE 14

At the same time, the third version changes the original left hand so that it takes on the key sssl rhythm of the piece—the opening rhythm of Beethoven's Fifth Symphony—while stretching the chord to make it more virtuosic.

EXAMPLE 15

Every detail of the original is reconceived. The repeated note of version 1 becomes more interesting in version 2, and what was originally a simple downward scale becomes quirkier and more difficult to play. Finally, the simple arpeggio that ends version 1 gets compressed and swoops up and down the keyboard in a blur almost faster than the ear can follow in version 3.

EXAMPLE 16

When all of these small surface changes accumulate, the simple original version of example 14 becomes this thrilling version:

EXAMPLE 17

The key point here is that Liszt is not simply arranging or decorating an earlier piece of piano music but rather translating it gesture by gesture into what is in fact a brand-new medium: the medium of the nineteenth-century virtuoso piano. Once the main ideas of the original exercise have been translated into "transcendental language," Liszt starts to work with and develop them in fantastically inventive ways. One example will suffice to illustrate the overall approach. The introduction, you remember, was based on a simple thumb melody of repeated E's. Transposed higher, these E's become A's. With a repeated-note pattern divided between the hands underneath, we get this seemingly fresh idea.

EXAMPLE 18

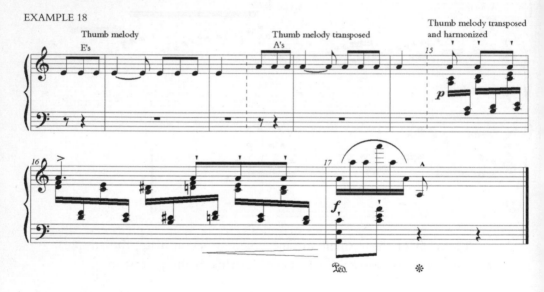

Once Liszt has created this idea, it rises higher and higher and begins to be developed.

EXAMPLE 19

[continued]

EXAMPLE 19 [continued]

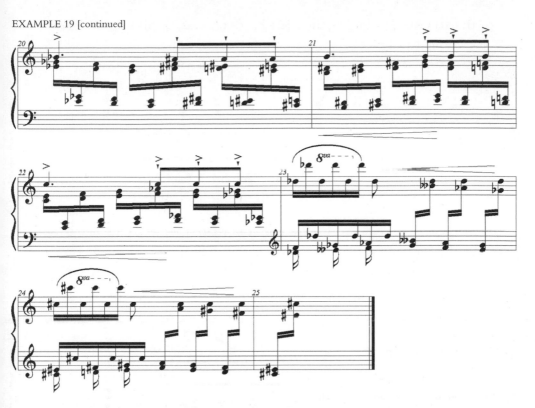

This process of taking simple materials and reconceiving them within a new pianistic vocabulary is at the heart of Liszt's approach to composition. The later versions of the *Transcendental* Études transform Liszt's original 1823 versions in much the same way as his operatic paraphrases transform the originals they are based on. Liszt was an omnivorous translator, taking whatever music came his way—operas, symphonies, songs, Hungarian dances, or even his own early works—and translating it into the language of the modern virtuoso piano. The A-minor *Transcendental* Étude uses the earlier exercise as a springboard for an exploration of pianistic possibilities, and Liszt develops and combines his teenage material in fantastically imaginative ways throughout the piece. However, like a savvy performer intent on generating thunderous applause, Liszt saves his most dazzling tricks for last, and the ending of this étude is astonishing.

An enormous number of Liszt's virtuosic effects depend on the simple idea of octave equivalence (the idea that all C's or E's on a piano are essentially "equivalent"—that is, the same note). If I keep all of Liszt's notes but switch octaves to put the notes close together, the passage that begins the coda becomes easy to play but not very exciting to listen to.

EXAMPLE 20

Liszt, however, puts the first chord in each measure in a low octave in the left hand and a high octave in the right hand, and the daredevil leap on each downbeat is thrilling to listen to, though terrifying to play.

EXAMPLE 21

Similarly, rearranging the next passage in close position makes it effortless to play.

EXAMPLE 22

However, putting these same notes in different octaves with leaps every other beat turns this simple idea into a passage that is as thrilling to watch as it is to listen to.

Finally, the ending of the étude—Liszt creatively misreading Beethoven—is spectacular. The left hand repeats the same three-note

EXAMPLE 23

pattern (A–D–D♯) five times, each time refusing to resolve. The three notes then repeat slower, stretched out rhythmically. Then just the first two notes—the A and the D—and finally, after a pause, a resolution. Above all of this, the right hand keeps repeating the same three chords in different positions, higher and higher, and louder and louder, until the piece ends where it began—with our thumb motive, the repeated E's. Beethoven's famous Fifth-Symphony rhythm, transformed over three decades and three versions into Liszt's extraordinary A-Minor *Transcendental* Étude.

EXAMPLE 24

[continued]

EXAMPLE 24 [continued]

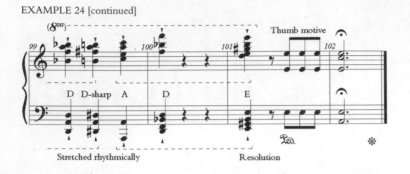

The Medium Is the Message

In a sense, the three different versions of the *Transcendental* Études reflect, in microcosm, the artistic and social history of the keyboard étude. In the Baroque and Classical-period world, instruction was the principal purpose of keyboard exercises. Bach's harpsichord exercises were primarily meant for private study and private meditation for both composers and performers, and piano exercises like Czerny's provided finger training for aspiring pianists. Liszt's original 1826 exercises grow out of this tradition, but by the 1830s, music for the new nineteenth-century piano was becoming public. Concert études like the *Transcendental* Études perfectly captured the opportunity of this "zeitgeist moment" by exploiting the new instrument's possibilities in its new artistic setting—the public concert hall—in the hands of a new class of performers: the touring keyboard virtuosos. Liszt's études have nothing to do with private study or instruction and everything to do with virtuosic public display.

Conceiving and reconceiving material in terms of the possibilities offered by the modern piano was the starting point for Liszt's imaginative genius, and the surface of the music is where his astonishing originality lives. His piano transcriptions of the nine Beethoven symphonies and Berlioz's *Symphonie Fantastique* are among the most famous piano transcriptions ever written. These pieces don't just take the notes of these symphonies and arrange them for the keyboard; they completely reconceive them in the world of the virtuoso piano. In the same way, Liszt's second and third versions of the *Transcendental* Études are really transcriptions of his own first versions. Liszt's least successful transcriptions are the ones that are the most respectful and conservative. Fidelity to the original source material is irrelevant in a Lisztian recital. Virtuosic transformation is all that matters.

Liszt arrived on the scene at a unique moment in history shaped by a rising middle class, public concerts, ubiquitous pianos, and touring keyboard virtuosos, and at this moment in time, the surface of the music could become the music. To borrow Marshall McLuhan's famous phrase, the medium became the message. In many pieces of Bach, musical ideas exist almost independent of their instrumental setting. A work like *The Art of Fugue* could be composed as pure music, without even specifying its exact instrumentation. But in Liszt, the instrument and its possibilities are everything. A musical idea is inseparable from its instrumental realization.

Utilizing the full potential of new mediums and surfaces is at the heart of Liszt's and Chopin's legacy. We take it for granted today that if you're going to say something artistically, the medium in which you say it—be it piano, feature film, television, book, CD, or DVD—plays a major role in determining what can be said. New mediums create new forms of expression, and expression is medium-specific. The nineteenth-century piano created a universe of sounds whose possibilities are still being explored by composers to this very day. Liszt's and Chopin's piano, and the music they wrote for it, created a richly expressive, virtuosic medium whose message is still being written.

[11]

Felix Mendelssohn
(1809–1847)
Scherzo from the String Octet
in E-flat Major, Op. 20

There is one god—Bach—and Mendelssohn is his prophet.

—HECTOR BERLIOZ

The Greatest Child Prodigy?

If you were to ask concertgoers to name the greatest compositional prodigy in the history of classical music, surely the most common answer would be Mozart. However, in terms of pure quality, a convincing case could be made that this distinction belongs to Mendelssohn, not to Mozart. To be sure, no one composed more music at an early age than Mozart. As I mentioned earlier, Mozart started composing simple keyboard pieces at age five, progressed to violin sonatas and orchestral music at six and seven, and wrote his first symphony at age nine. However, his first mature pieces date from his late-teenage years, and he really did not start composing his greatest music until he was in his twenties. Mendelssohn—a late bloomer by Mozart's standards—did not begin composing until he was ten, but the octet written when he was sixteen and the *Overture to a Midsummer Night's Dream* written a year later are

mature masterpieces that go far beyond anything that Mozart or anyone else had ever composed at a comparable age.

If you look closely into Mendelssohn's biography (R. Larry Todd's is
the excellent, definitive reference), you quickly realize that these teenage
masterpieces were anything but a fluke. Mendelssohn's compositional
training between the ages of ten and seventeen under the conservative
German composer Carl Zelter was unbelievably rigorous. At the age of
ten, Mendelssohn began to write figured-bass exercises in three and four
parts, followed by chorales in four and five parts. By the age of eleven
he had started to write invertible counterpoint and canon in two and
three parts and fugue in two and three parts. By the time he was twelve,
he had already written more than thirty fugues in his exercise book.
Given Zelter's reactionary outlook, Bach was always the model, and
Mendelssohn wrote fugues, double fugues, triple fugues, and fugues
with chorales as if he were an eighteenth-century musician training to
become Bach's successor at Leipzig rather than the nineteenth-century
musician he was. He also, of course, wrote his own free compositions,
and between the ages of eleven and fourteen, he produced over a
hundred compositions in every conceivable medium, from keyboard
and chamber works to symphonies, concertos, lieder, and operas. The
great pianist Ignaz Moscheles summed up the matter when he said,
"Felix, a boy of fifteen, is a phenomenon. What are all prodigies as
compared with him? Gifted children, but nothing else. This Felix
Mendelssohn is already a mature artist, and yet but fifteen years old!"

Goethe without Words

Though the octet has become one of Mendelssohn's most famous
pieces, we know almost nothing about its origins except that it was
written as a birthday present for Mendelssohn's violin teacher and
friend, Eduard Rietz, and that it was completed on October 15, 1825.
The first performance took place that year in the Mendelssohn
household on Rietz's birthday, October 17, but the first public performance didn't take place until 1836, eleven years later, in the Leipzig
Gewandhaus, with Mendelssohn himself playing the second viola part.
Though all of the octet's four movements are extraordinary, the third-
movement scherzo is not only one of Mendelssohn's most famous
movements, it is also an example of a kind of writing that almost
defines the term "Mendelssohnian."

EXAMPLE 1

[continued]

EXAMPLE 1 [continued]

[continued]

EXAMPLE 1 [continued]

Scherzos, like minuets (see chapter 4), were traditionally written with three beats to a measure, and were normally made up of three sections—an opening scherzo section, a middle section called the trio, and a repeat of the opening scherzo. In his string octet, however, Mendelssohn reinvents the scherzo as a movement with only two beats to a measure and no trio or middle section. According to Fanny, Felix's sister, in the scherzo of the octet, Felix

> set to music the stanza from the Walpurgis-night Dream in "Faust":—"The flight of the clouds and the veil of mist / Are lighted from above. / A breeze in the leaves, a wind in the reeds, /And all has vanished." To me alone he told this idea: the whole piece is to be played *staccato* and *pianissimo*, the *tremulandos* coming in now and then, the trills passing away with the quickness of lightning; everything new and strange, and at the same time most insinuating and pleasing, one feels so near the world of spirits, carried away in the air, half inclined to snatch up a broomstick

and follow the aerial procession. At the end the first violin takes a flight with a featherlike lightness, and—all has vanished.

The writing in this opening would be superb for a composer of any age, but for a sixteen-year-old it is almost unbelievable. All eight string parts are completely independent. The four fast repeating notes in the second violin and the first viola give energy and excitement to the passage (measures 1 through 4). The *pizzicato* cello line holds the music together, and the way the cello accelerates in the third and fourth measure perfectly matches the way the four-note melody (x) is shortened to its last two notes (1/2x) with an added trill to increase the excitement.

As the phrase continues, the technique becomes even more sophisticated, and the pace of the compositional thought is breathtaking. While the first and second violins are playing the main melody—"y"— the two violas are doing it upside-down (that is, "4-notes-go-**down**-then-circle-**down**" becomes "4-notes-go-**up**-then-circle-**up**"). The violins then repeat the idea higher, and before you can catch your breath, a new closing idea ("z") finishes the phrase as the cello switches excitedly to faster bowed notes to push to the cadence at measure 9. That a sixteen-year-old could write music with this kind of lightness of touch, rhythmic energy, transparent instrumental texture, and effortless craftsmanship is almost unbelievable, and this opening phrase is a perfect example of the new kind of expression Mendelssohn brought to the world of Romantic chamber music.

Mendelssohn was almost constitutionally incapable of simply repeating a passage identically, so when the movement's opening idea returns in measure 9, he adds a new, fantastic little repeated-note accompaniment figure—violins imitating toy trumpets ("r")—which passes through the parts from third violin to fourth violin to second cello. As if this isn't enough, he then puts the opening melody in the cello and viola on the bottom of the instrumental texture while switching from a minor key to a major key! As in so much of the octet, Mendelssohn seems to take an almost childlike delight in his own compositional virtuosity, as if he is as thrilled and amazed by his own technical prowess as we are. The piece is literally bursting with detail, and Mendelssohn's completely unself-conscious joy in his own abilities and musical discoveries gives the octet an extraordinary exuberance and vitality.

As we have seen over and over again in this book, the difference between good and great is both enormous and infinitesimal. It is hundreds of small, inspired choices made by a composer—note by note, rhythm by rhythm, and measure by measure—and the next phrase is a perfect example. To help make Mendelssohn's genius clear, I have written a version of measures 17 through 20 that keeps all of his notes but changes one rhythm.

My version, like Mendelssohn's, passes a three-note scale idea ("a") through the ensemble, followed by a repeated-note idea ("b") that closes the thought. The whole combination happens twice, first moving from high to low instrumentally, then from low to high. My version changes only the rhythm of "b." It is "almost Mendelssohn." Good, not great. Mendelssohn's version, however, speeds up "b"— the repeated-note idea—twice as fast, and as a result of this one small change, we are suddenly in the "world of spirits." These fast little *tremulandos* change everything and instantly give the passage its hovering, spritelike quality; however, the compositional thought is

EXAMPLE 2A

EXAMPLE 2B

moving so fast, the listener barely has time to let the moment register. An instant later the passage repeats lower (measures 21 through
24, example 1), with, as always, more changes to process, but before
we have time to savor these details, we suddenly find ourselves at the
scherzo's wonderful second theme.

Second Theme

The moment this new theme begins, we realize that the sixteen-
year-old Mendelssohn has been thinking ahead of us all along, as the
three-note idea ("a") that passed through the parts in the previous
phrase now becomes the core of the movement's fairylike second
theme ("s").

EXAMPLE 3

[continued]

EXAMPLE 3 [continued]

The effortlessness of Mendelssohn's compositional technique in this section is simply astonishing. The music shifts to a major key, and all of the instruments have the same rhythm for the first time in the movement, giving this second theme a focused, playful quality. Its short, two-measure melody is repeated once with different harmony and is then copied higher (measures 29 and 30) as the descending cello line gives the passage direction and shape. Then, in an extraordinary moment, as the cello completes its descending scale, instead of resolving it as expected in measure 31, Mendelssohn magically veers off to a surprising D-major chord. Suddenly, in this unexpected key, the fast repeating notes from the opening of the movement return in the violas (measure 31), underneath the opening melody (measure 33), but now the sustained chords in the lower instruments give this material a kind of glowing serenity utterly different from the restless energy of the opening. As always, Mendelssohn's compositional thought races ahead at lightning speed, and before we know it, he has altered the ending of the melody to bring the music back to reality—back to the fairylike second theme—for a repeat of the entire section with wonderful changes of detail in every measure.

This superbly crafted, elfin second theme is a prime example of what Mendelssohn is all about. The writing is supremely accomplished, and everything is lighter than air, delicately shaded, graceful, and filled with rhythmic life and inventive detail. The returns of the opening theme are a wonderful surprise, and within seconds, a passage that comes directly out of the kind of two-part counterpoint exercises Mendelssohn worked on with Zelter brings us to the ending of the exposition. It begins by passing two contrasted ideas—a scale and a leap—through three groups of instruments until a unison passage gradually brings all eight instruments together to end the exposition.

EXAMPLE 4

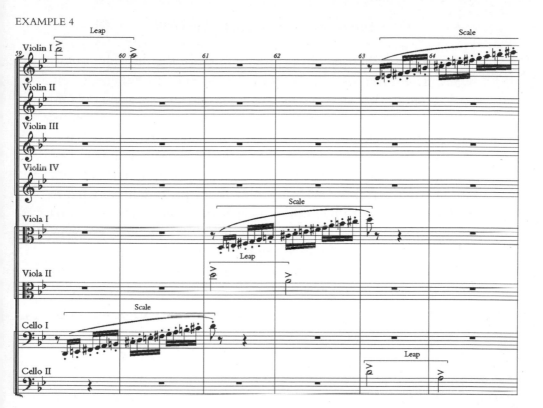

Development and Return

Like nearly every nineteenth-century composer, Mendelssohn was in awe of Beethoven, and it is Beethoven's scherzos, with their sonata-like exposition-development-recapitulation structure, that are the formal models for Mendelssohn's scherzos. Mendelssohn's mastery of Beethoven's developmental technique at the age of sixteen is remarkable. The development section of the octet's scherzo begins by transposing the unison idea that ended the exposition into several different keys. Then, in a classic Mendelssohn moment, this unison figure suddenly turns out to be not the melody but rather the accompaniment to a new, flowing theme in longer notes in violin 3. Transforming this unison idea into an accompaniment not only changes our understanding of its fundamental meaning, it also changes and slows down the rhythmic pulse of the entire section.

EXAMPLE 5

[continued]

EXAMPLE 5 [continued]

To really give you a chance to appreciate the teenage Mendelssohn's remarkable technique and hear all of the complexities that race by at blistering speed, I want to build up the next passage in two steps. Two simple ideas are at the heart of the phrase—a little turn figure (a note decorated by the notes above and below), and a trill with a resolution that I call "trill-flip." Removing all of the other notes, it is easy to follow these two ideas as they flash from instrument to instrument.

EXAMPLE 6

However, when the turn figure is extended, the key changes every four measures, and the other parts are added, it becomes an exhilarating challenge to try to keep up with the complexity and speed of Mendelssohn's dazzling technique.

EXAMPLE 7

The passage that prepares us for the return of the opening music is full of surprises, and it is a classic example of Mendelssohn's "creatively misreading" Beethoven. It begins with the "trill-flip" idea going wild in the first violin, and then in classic Mendelssohn/Beethoven fashion reduces the idea to its last two measures (measure 125). This connects seamlessly with a new, poignant, scale idea—"c" (measures 127 and 128) that is immediately repeated and transposed higher. Suddenly, in a shocking moment, the harmony shifts (measure 135), and the opening accompaniment and opening melodic fragment of the movement return in the wrong key. Four surprising measures correct the "mistake," and before we know it, the opening of the movement returns in the correct key with a satisfying sense of both surprise and inevitability.

EXAMPLE 8

[continued]

EXAMPLE 8 [continued]

[continued]

EXAMPLE 8 [continued]

[continued]

EXAMPLE 8 [continued]

As in a "normal" Beethoven scherzo, all the material of the opening scherzo section returns; however, nearly all of it is transformed in some way. A brand-new "fairy-music" transition section that contrasts *legato* and *staccato* now leads to the second theme, and the theme itself is in the lower strings, not the upper strings this time, as if grandfather fairies have replaced the original adolescent sprites.

EXAMPLE 9

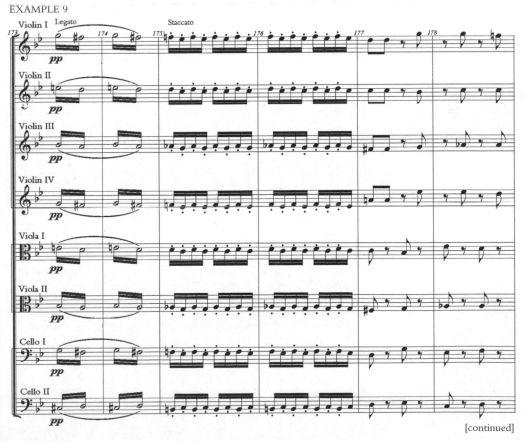

[continued]

EXAMPLE 9 [continued]

To conclude the movement, Mendelssohn returns to the unison music that ended the exposition, but now the material is developed and extended from four measures to eighteen until, as Fanny put it, "at the end the first violin takes a flight with a featherlike lightness,

EXAMPLE 10

[continued]

EXAMPLE 10 [continued]

and—all has vanished." The piece dissolves into thin air as the first violin's arpeggio floats into the ether, as if the whole thing were nothing but a midsummer night's dream.

The Mendelssohn Mystery

Though Mendelssohn would go on to write many other important works in his tragically short career—he died at the age of thirty-eight—none would be greater than his two teenage masterpieces, the octet and the *Overture to a Midsummer Night's Dream*, and for more than 160 years people have wondered why. Did Mendelssohn's astonishingly busy performing career as the nineteenth-century's first superstar conductor and pianist take too much time and creative energy away from his composing? Did he, as Charles Rosen suggests, simply lose the youthful sense of daring he had as a teenager as he became a more self-aware adult? Or did the rigorous, conservative training that gave him the technique to be able to write these masterpieces at such a young age ultimately limit his ability to respond to the rapid changes of the modern musical world as he grew up? Did he, as Berlioz famously suggested, "love the dead too much"?

It was no coincidence that it was Mendelssohn who almost single-handedly brought Bach back to life for the nineteenth century when he conducted his famous revival of Bach's *Saint Matthew Passion* in 1829. Throughout his life, Mendelssohn was referred to, as Brahms would be a generation later, as the "Classical Romantic"; however, in the octet, his reverence for the music of the dead—Bach and Mozart in particular—was freeing, not imprisoning. The octet was written at the perfect moment in Mendelssohn's life: when he had internalized a deep, technical, compositional knowledge of the past yet still had the youthful daring and confidence to appropriate it and use it for his own ends. At the age of sixteen, he was aware of the past but not intimidated by it. The work is a reminder that though much of the rhetoric and attention of the Romantic Era focused on revolutionary composers like Wagner, Liszt, and Berlioz, there was also a long line of conservative composers, beginning with Mendelssohn and extending through Brahms, Dvořák, and Bruckner, who found the music and craft of the past to be an inspiration to creativity, not a hindrance.

At the end of his life, Mendelssohn declared his string octet to be his favorite of all his works, and his judgment could not be more on the mark. No composer has ever written a greater piece of music at a younger age. Mendelssohn, not Mozart, was the greatest compositional prodigy in history.

[12]

Richard Wagner
(1813–1883)
Prelude to *Tristan and Isolde*

—————

I believe in God, Mozart and Beethoven, and likewise their disciples and apostles; I believe in the Holy Spirit and the truth of the one, indivisible Art; - I believe that this Art proceeds from God, and lives within the hearts of all illumined men; - I believe that he who once has bathed in the sublime delights of this high Art, is consecrate to Her for ever, and never can deny Her; - I believe that through Art all men are saved.

—RICHARD WAGNER

Opera and Drama

With the exception of Beethoven, Wagner was probably the most influential composer of the nineteenth century. As single-minded compositionally as Chopin, Wagner wrote all his most important works for the theater, yet the impact of his revolutionary musical language was felt by composers working in every genre, and his influence extended beyond the world of music to literature, philosophy, and the visual arts. In purely operatic terms, his principal achievement was the creation of a new form—the music drama. The standard operas of the time were almost completely focused on singing, with the libretto serving as a kind of simple framework for the music; however, for Wagner, drama and music were one. As historian Donald Grout puts it, "The two were organically connected expressions of a single dramatic idea." This central belief in the unity of music and drama is at the heart of Wagner's entire theatrical approach, and he was the only major opera composer to write all of his librettos himself. In addition, the orchestra, which was largely an accompaniment to the voice in most nineteenth-century operas, became a principal dramatic agent in Wagner's works. For Wagner, the vocal lines of his operas are simply another element in the orchestral texture, and the whole traditional operatic structure of arias, recitatives, and set pieces is almost completely discarded in favor of a much more continuous, dramatic, narrative flow. Wagner's intense preoccupation with the fusing of drama and music reaches its most profound expression in his idea of the *Gesamtkunstwerk*, or universal artwork, in which words, stage setting, costumes, lighting, action, and music all combine to express the central drama of an opera, and the extraordinary theater Wagner built in Bayreuth to house his works in their perfect acoustical setting takes this dramatic obsession into the realm of architecture as well. Wagner's vision of opera as a kind of theater in which all of the art forms would contribute to a drama of significant content, epic scope, and unprecedented intensity had an enormous influence in the nineteenth century, and the power and influence of his vision remains undiminished today.

On a purely musical level, there are two principal innovations in Wagner's operas that significantly impacted other composers. The first was Wagner's idea of the leitmotif. The term itself was coined by Wagner's friend Hans von Wolzogen to describe the way Wagner represents characters, situations, objects, or ideas in his operas through recurring musical motifs or themes—for example, the leitmotif of the Ring, Fate, the Rainbow Bridge, or the Sword. These leitmotifs are usually heard in the orchestra at the first appearance of the object, idea, or situation and return at each subsequent reappearance, and they have generally been given arbitrary names drawn from the text at their first appearance. However, these leitmotifs are much more than mere musical labels. Like the motives or themes of a symphony, they return throughout the work in varied forms and in different musical contexts, and the meaning of a particular leitmotif deepens and develops as the drama progresses. In addition, a leitmotif may return to reflect a subconscious thought in the mind of a character even when the object itself is not part of the scene. Ultimately, the leitmotifs become part of the core musical material of the work, and because they have a built-in dramatic association, musical and dramatic development become intertwined in a powerful new way.

In addition to Wagner's purely operatic innovations, the extraordinary musical language that he developed in his later works had a profound influence on the entire musical language of the nineteenth century. Some composers imitated it, others rebelled against it, but almost no one was immune to its effect. Of all of Wagner's works, *Tristan and Isolde* is perhaps the most perfect embodiment of this revolutionary, chromatic musical language, and though no excerpt, least of all a purely instrumental excerpt, can do more than hint at the way this gargantuan four-hour masterpiece works, the opera's magnificent prelude is an excellent point of entry into many of the most important aspects of Wagner's mature style.

The Music of Delayed Gratification

While at work on the single largest musical project of the nineteenth century, the four enormous operas that make up the epic Ring of the Nibelung, Wagner became fascinated by the medieval legend of Tristan and Isolde. It is possible that this tale of forbidden love had a personal resonance for Wagner as at the time, he was in love with Mathilde Wesendonck, the wife of his chief financial patron, Otto Wesendonck, but whatever the reason, Wagner put aside work on his Ring cycle to compose *Tristan and Isolde* between 1857 and 1859. The opening of the opera's prelude is one of the most famous beginnings in all music, and Wagner described its tone in a highly emotional program note: "There is henceforth no end to the yearning, longing, rapture, and misery of love: world, power, fame, honor, chivalry, loyalty, and friendship, scattered like an insubstantial dream; one thing alone left living: longing, longing unquenchable, desire forever renewing itself, craving and languishing; one sole redemption: death, surcease of being, the sleep that knows no waking!"

If a single word could describe the heart of this enormous four-hour opera, it would be the word Wagner repeats three times in this quotation—*longing*. The music's continual lack of resolution perfectly expresses the longing and agony suffered by the lovers over the course of the opera, and everything in the prelude contributes to conveying their anguish. From the opera's first note, the glacially slow tempo stretches out and surreally heightens the effect of each musical gesture, and the piece's mythic timescale is established by the end of the first three measures, which take almost a half a minute to complete.

EXAMPLE 1

The slow-motion pacing of the prelude gives each musical event an extraordinary focus and power. The opening *crescendo* in the cello (the four-note leitmotif traditionally labeled "Sorrow" or "Longing") takes nearly ten seconds to complete and creates enormous intensity as the sound grows. When the famous "Tristan chord" finally arrives (measure 2), its dissonant melody note lasts for a full five seconds without resolution and then yearns upward until all of the voices finally wash out on a dominant-seventh chord (E7) at the end of measure3. This kind of chromatic writing in which multiple, overlapping voices head at different speeds toward an arrival point—almost invariably a dominant chord—which itself refuses to resolve is at the heart of Wagner's style, as are the dissonances the independent voices create along the way.

Yet as superb as these opening three measures are in conveying the opera's sense of unfulfilled desire, what follows is even more striking. Having finally reached a dominant chord in measure 3, we desperately want it to resolve to an A chord—the home chord of the prelude. (Though the size, language, and scope of the two works could not be more different, compare this opening with Chopin's A-minor Mazurka, which also begins on a striking dissonance and refuses to resolve to its home chord for twenty measures.) However, in shocking fashion, instead of a resolution, Wagner gives us silence. At the prelude's incredibly slow tempo, this silence lasts for almost eight full seconds. For a conductor, the temptation to beat through these rests quickly and get on to the next phrase is almost irresistible, but this seemingly endless silence is central to the piece's expression and finally leads not to resolution, but instead to a repeat of the whole opening, copied higher. These first seven measures of music take nearly a minute to wash out on two dominant-seventh chords (E7 and G7), both of which refuse to resolve.

In terms of resolution, from here on things only get worse. The opening gesture, with a slight variation in the melody, begins to repeat a third time, still higher, arriving on yet a third dominant-seventh chord (B7). Perhaps, we hope, this third attempt will lead to a resolution; however, after yet another dramatic silence, Wagner instead repeats measures 10 and 11 ("Desire/Yearning") an octave higher. Then, in a superb theatrical moment, Wagner narrows the focus of the drama by reducing "Desire/Yearning" to its final two notes (E♯, F♯) without accompaniment. The two notes *crescendo* twice, desperately trying to find a resolution as the tension becomes almost unbearable (measures 14 and 15). Then, in a thrilling moment, horns, strings, and woodwinds enter *forte*, harmonizing these two notes with a rich, voluptuous chord (the E7 chord of measure 3) as the two notes expand to become a motive traditionally called "Tristan's Anguish." Finally, almost two minutes into the piece, as the music swells to *fortissimo*, on the brink of resolution, instead of resolving to the home chord (A) that we have been waiting for since measure 3, Wagner resolves to an F chord instead. This "deceptive cadence" (for non-musicians, a cadence in which an unexpected chord is "deceptively" substituted for the expected chord of resolution) is the quintessential Tristan cadence. It *is* Tristan's anguish—Wagner's musical equivalent of unresolved yearning and longing—and deceptive cadences like this one become the basic cadence type for the entire opera.

"The Glance"

I mentioned earlier that one of the key ways Wagner structured his operas was through the use and reuse of leitmotifs, and the next phrase beautifully illustrates this technique. The five-note motive that begins in measure 17 (see score) is traditionally labeled "The Look," or "The Glance," referring to the look between the two lovers that initially caused Isolde to spare Tristan's life. The first thing to notice about this exquisite motive in the cello is the way it emerges seamlessly out of the preceding music, beginning with the cadence's melody note (an A) as the deceptive cadence is finishing in measure 17. Like so many Wagnerian leitmotifs, "The Glance" is brief—just five notes—yet it captures the emotional essence of the moment through its hesitating, dotted rhythm and its yearning leap. As the passage continues, Wagner's treatment of the idea is remarkably fluid and organic. As I mentioned earlier, these leitmotifs are not mere labels but rather motivic germs. Wagner states the motive of "The Glance" once, but then immediately begins to vary, develop, and extend it with ever-increasing intensity (see score). Though we cannot know it yet, this four-measure unit (from the second half of measure 17 to the first half of measure 21) will ultimately become a key structural building block in both the prelude and the opera. All we can know at this point is that the variations on the rhythm of "The Glance" build in intensity and lead to the first real harmonic resolution of the piece, as the A-major chord we have been waiting for since measure 3 ends the first section of the prelude (compare this to Chopin's A-Minor Mazurka, measure 20).

"The Love Potion"

As is so often the case in *Tristan*, this rare moment of resolution (measure 24) is incredibly brief and lasts for only a quarter note before the music moves on to another key and a motive traditionally called "The Love Potion." Though all of the leitmotifs in this prelude have been given discrete labels and function as independent ideas, it is important to notice their resemblances to one another as it is these musical similarities that allow the different motives to combine and flow together so effortlessly. (For example, the leap and dotted rhythm of "The Love Potion" come from "The Glance.") Wagner is not literally deriving these motives from each other à la Beethoven, but instead working with ideas whose shapes feel organically connected in ways that give unity to the musical flow.

Working with leitmotifs allows Wagner to create rich, multilayered dramatic textures, and the next phrase is a perfect example. The passage begins with the beautiful "Love Potion" motive (notice the heartrending chords of measure 25 and the second chord of measure 26), which is then repeated lower in measures 27 and 28. Yet as this second statement is finishing, the basses and bassoons (the lowest voice in the left hand of the piano reduction) ominously proclaim the motive of "Death" or "Fate." Rarely have love and death been linked more intimately or more explicitly, and one of the glories of Wagner's style is his ability to work on multiple psychological and emotional levels at the same time through orchestral textures made up of several different leitmotifs.

The entrance of death or fate into the musical narrative darkens the glow of the "Love Potion" music, and after two failed tries at resolution, Wagner seamlessly slips into a return of the music of "The Glance" (measure 32). Repeating a unit of music lets us know that it is important, and the first four measures of "The Glance" return intact until a new continuation—traditionally labeled "The Magic Casket"—changes the musical direction of the phrase. This is core Wagner technique. Though an individual leitmotif may consist of only a few notes, it is often an entire phrase of music generated by a leitmotif that becomes a key building block in an opera as it returns over and over again with different endings, taking the music in a new direction each time (unity/variety). This four-measure phrase generated by "The Glance" returns five times in the prelude, but each appearance is preceded and followed

by different music, and it is the entire phrase, not just the five-note leitmotif, that ultimately plays a central role in the climax of the piece.

EXAMPLE 2

"Deliverance by Death"

Once you have a feeling for the prelude's key leitmotifs, you can begin to see how Wagner knits them together to create larger paragraphs of music. The next minute and a half of the piece uses nothing but the music of "The Love Potion" and "The Glance" (see score), but each appearance begins in an unexpected way and ends with a new continuation or development of the original material. The section builds in intensity and volume until an arrival on an E pedal point in measure 63 ushers in the prelude's central section and final new leit-motif—"Deliverance by Death."

The next twenty-two measures form one extraordinary *crescendo* to the climax of the piece, and the overwhelming power and intensity of this music almost defines the term "Wagnerian." The leitmotif "Deliverance by Death" (measures 63 and 64) is typically short but striking, and it is made up of a sweeping scale, an arpeggio, and a two-note ending. (In the full orchestration, the sweeping scale in the strings is actually longer and contains more notes than in the piano reduction.) For labeling purposes, I will refer to each statement of "Deliverance by Death" by the top note of its scale—that is, I will call the first version of the motive "Deliverance by Death on A."

EXAMPLE 4

[continued]

EXAMPLE 4 [continued]

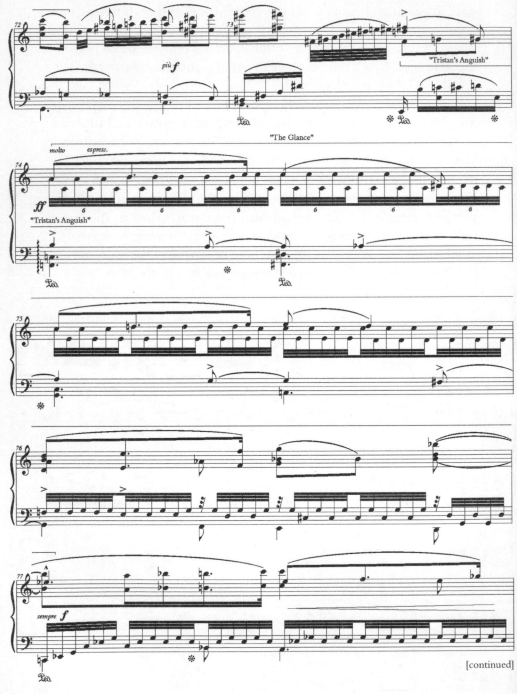

[continued]

EXAMPLE 4 [continued]

[continued]

EXAMPLE 4 [continued]

Stage 1

The way Wagner creates the prelude's shattering climax is as power-ful as it is simple. The build occurs in several stages. It starts with three statements of "Deliverance by Death" that are each a step higher and louder in volume—first on an A (measures 63 and 64), then on a B (measures 64 and 65), and then on a C-sharp with a slightly changed ending (measures 65 and 66). There is no more basic way to gener-ate musical excitement than to repeat an idea several times, each time louder and higher, and the effect is particularly striking when the idea begins with a sweeping scale like "Deliverance by Death."

Stage 2

The second stage of the *crescendo* begins as if to simply repeat the idea a fourth time, still another step higher, on a D; however, when the sweeping scale reaches its top note, the motive pauses to focus attention on the woodwinds, which ominously enter with "Desire/Yearning." The entrance of this darker motive shifts the tone of the entire section and adds another musical and dramatic layer to the texture. Wagner then alternates combinations of the two motives until an ecstatic version of "Deliverance by Death" rises even higher to F♯ (measure 69). Though it seems like these sweeping scales could not possibly rise any higher, one final climactic version, still higher, on A (measure 71), leads to the final phase of the build.

Stage 3

The last stage of this twenty-two-measure *crescendo* utilizes the full power of Wagner's leitmotif technique. The motive of "Tristan's Anguish" from measures 16 and 17 returns with great intensity in the full orchestra, and, in a thrilling musical overlap, completes its deceptive cadence as the music of "The Glance" enters in the string section (measure 74). The *fortissimo*, full-orchestra version of "The Glance" that follows is as rich and voluptuous in its harmony and orchestration as any music written in the nineteenth century, and after copying the original version for three full measures (measures 74 through 76), Wagner alters its ending to begin the final push to climax.

Though the complexity of this climax can only be hinted at in the piano reduction of example 4, its overpowering effect is clearly audible. "Glance-derived" scales in the violins rise higher and higher, and woodwinds and brass gradually thicken the texture until finally the prelude's four principal leitmotifs dramatically combine (with the help of rolling timpani) to lead to a shattering climax on a *fortissimo* Tristan chord in measure 83. No one had ever written an intense, overwhelming, erotic climax like this before, but equally startling is its lack of resolution. As the violins shudder downward and the orchestra thins out, "Desire/Yearning" returns in the oboe in its original form (measure 83), still without resolution. The only possible resolution of the desire and yearning that this chord represents lies in death, and only at the end of the opera, some four hours later, do "Desire/Yearning" and the Tristan chord finally resolve in stunning fashion as Isolde dies and the curtain falls.

EXAMPLE 5

Epilogue

Though there are still some three minutes of music left in the prelude, for all practical purposes the rest of the piece is an exhausted epilogue. There is no new material. The original motives—"Sorrow," "Desire/ Yearning," "The Glance," and "The Magic Casket"—return with slight variation in new transpositions and combinations, but none of these developments is compositionally significant. All forward momentum has been frustrated, and resolution is nowhere to be found. Emotionally and dramatically, there is nothing but longing and yearning. Finally, to prepare for Scene I, the opening six measures return slightly reharmonized to shift the music toward the key of the opening scene, and the prelude ends as quietly as it began with two *pianissimo*, *pizzicato* G's in the bass and cello.

EXAMPLE 6

It is surely not surprising that *Tristan and Isolde* initially provoked extremely negative reactions. The July 5, 1865, edition of the *Allgemeine musikalische Zeitung* said:

Not to mince words, it is the glorification of sensual pleasure, tricked out with every titillating device, it is unremitting materialism, according to which human beings have no higher destiny than, after living the life of turtle doves, "to vanish in sweet odours, like a breath." In the service of this end, music has been enslaved to the word; the most ideal of the Muses has been made to grind the colours for indecent paintings . . . We think that the stage presentation of the poem *Tristan and Isolde* amounts to an act of indecency. Wagner does not show us the life of heroes of Nordic sagas which would edify and strengthen the spirit of his German audiences. What he does present is the ruination of the life of heroes through sensuality.

The critic and Brahms supporter Eduard Hanslick in 1868 said that the *Tristan* Prelude "reminds one of the old Italian painting of a martyr whose intestines are slowly unwound from his body on a reel," and in typically blunt fashion, Robert Schumann's wife, Clara, wrote that *Tristan and Isolde* was "the most repugnant thing [she had] ever seen or heard in all [her] life."

As time passed, however, opinions began to change. Verdi said that he "stood in wonder and terror" before Wagner's *Tristan*, and after hearing the work as a student in 1889, the conductor Bruno Walter said, "Never before has my soul been deluged with such floods of sound and passion, never had my heart been consumed by such yearning and sublime bliss . . . A new epoch had begun: Wagner was my god, and I wanted to become his prophet." Even Richard Strauss, who initially despised the work and claimed that Wagner's music "would kill a cat and would turn rocks into scrambled eggs from fear of [its] hideous discords," eventually changed his mind and later wrote, "*Tristan and Isolde* marked the end of all romanticism. Here the yearning of the entire 19th century is gathered in one focal point."

Perhaps it was inevitable that the magnitude and scope of Wagner's achievement would provoke extreme reactions. Surely his unbridled egotism, virulent anti-Semitism, and personal and professional immorality contributed to this polarization of opinion, yet in spite of his horrific qualities as a human being, his accomplishments as a composer were and are simply too enormous to be ignored. Works like *Tristan* and the Ring Cycle changed music history forever. They were the beginning of the end for the world of traditional tonality. Huge stretches of *Tristan* lacked the kind of resolution and cohesive tonal center that had organized music for hundreds of years, and the harmonic language of Bruckner, Mahler, Strauss, Schoenberg, Berg, and Webern can all be traced back to the chromatic world of *Tristan*. Without Wagner, the history of nineteenth- and twentieth-century music would have been completely different. As the composer Paul Hindemith pointed out in 1937, "Not until the turn of the century did the outlines of the new world discovered in *Tristan* begin to take shape. Music reacted to it as a human body to an injected serum, which it at first strives to exclude as a poison, and only afterwards learns to accept as necessary and even wholesome." As we enter the second decade of the twenty-first century, the controversies over Wagner's music, writings, and politics show no signs of abating, and that is as it should be. Yet whatever our opinion on these matters, they should never blind us to the overwhelming power and stunning achievement of the Romantic period's greatest and most influential composer.

[13]

Giuseppe Verdi
(1813–1901)

"De' Miei Bollenti Spiriti"
from *La Traviata*

You may have the universe if I may have Italy.

—GIUSEPPE VERDI

Music and Drama

Verdi was without a doubt the single most important Italian composer of the second half of the nineteenth century. His remarkable career spanned some fifty-five years—his first opera was staged in 1839 and his last in 1893—and with the exception of his *Requiem* and several minor works, all of his music was written for the stage. There is probably no operatic composer who has contributed more works to the standard operatic repertoire than Verdi, and at least twenty of his twenty-six operas are still heard in opera houses today. In terms of focus, Verdi was a match for the century's other central opera composer, Wagner, but in every other way their approaches could not have been more different. Verdi was completely uninterested in the mythological symbolism at the heart of Wagner's operas, and he had no interest in Wagner's radical chromaticism, "unending melody," and orchestrally dominated vocal writing. The principal focus of opera for Verdi, which remained unchanged throughout his entire career, was human drama expressed through direct, emotional vocal melody.

When Verdi worked with singers, he would always ask them to think about the drama first, then the music. He told Felice Varesi, the first to sing the title role in Verdi's *Macbeth*, "Study closely the dramatic situation and the words: the music comes of itself." When he was writing *Don Carlo* he said, "Give me a libretto and the opera is written." For Verdi an opera began when a story and words gripped him, and he involved himself in every aspect of the theatrical enterprise, working exhaustively not only on the libretto of an opera but also on the costumes, lighting, sets, and props. In his search for intense, heightened emotional expression, dramatic truth was far more important than actual truth, and no work more powerfully distorts reality in its search for emotional truth than his most famous opera, *La Traviata*.

From Fact to Fiction: *La Traviata*

La Traviata, literally "The Women Who Strayed," was premiered in 1853, and it was Verdi's only work that might be said to be "ripped from the day's headlines." The opera was based on real events that everyone in the audience was aware of, but those events were passed through three filtering lenses. Violetta, the heroine of the opera, was actually Marie Duplessis, a courtesan who had come to Paris at the age of fifteen, risen to the top of her profession, and died of consumption at the age of twenty-three, six years before the opera's premiere. The writer Alexandre Dumas was one of her lovers (as was his father), but Marie rejected him in order to marry a richer admirer, and she died shortly thereafter. Dumas was crushed and went on a trip, during which he tried unsuccessfully to forget her. When he returned, he decided to write a novel about her, and within three weeks completed *Camille*. The novel not only changed Marie's name to Marguerite Gautier, it also began her transformation from the self-centered, ruthless exploiter of rich men she was to a romantic, sick girl who gives up the man she loves so as not to bring disgrace on his family. Not a word of this was true, yet it made for a wildly successful novel in 1847 and an equally successful, even more romanticized play that Verdi saw in 1852, a year before writing his opera. Verdi's version, with a libretto by Francesco Piave, romanticized this already fictionalized version even further, and though it bore no resemblance to reality, this is the version that has been imprinted on history.

"De' Miei Bollenti Spiriti": The Art of the *Crescendo*

Whether dealing with fact or fiction, a great opera composer, like a quick-sketch artist, must be able to create a scene, a mood, or a character in an instant. As Act II of *La Traviata* begins, Alfredo and Violetta have fallen in love and are living together out of wedlock. The action takes place, according to Verdi's stage directions (which he insisted be published word-for-word everywhere his operas were performed), in a country house near Paris. The scene starts with action as Alfredo enters in hunting clothes, and the music perfectly captures the bustle of his entry.

EXAMPLE 1

[continued]

EXAMPLE 1 [continued]

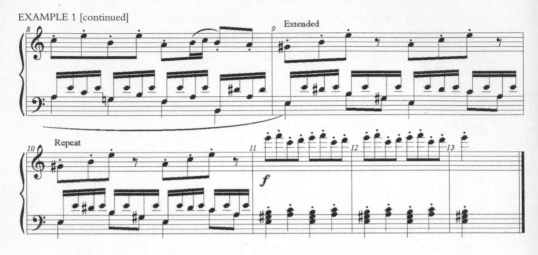

The music begins as if in midsentence, with no bass line, the same unstable chord that opened "Dove sono" (for musicians—a first-inversion chord), and fast notes in the accompaniment to create energy. As is so often the case with Verdi's music, the melodic idea is simple—a three-note figure ("a") repeated three times, each time lower—but the musical intensity of the phrase builds as it progresses. Verdi adds a bass line in measure 3, and increases the pacing of the harmony from two chords per measure to four chords per measure in measure 4, as the melody becomes more agitated as well. There is a wonderfully subtle harmonic moment as Verdi shifts back to C major to repeat the opening idea in measure 5, and this repeat further increases the music's intensity by extending the phrase and bringing in the full string section, *forte*, to end the orchestral introduction. In approximately twenty seconds, Alfredo's energy and character have been established, and the mood of the scene has been created before a single note has been sung.

For Verdi, the drama of opera was everything, and one of his life-long principles of dramatic construction, on the smallest and largest level, was what I will call the "*crescendo* principle." Though on a literal level a *crescendo* is simply a musical sign indicating an increase in volume, on a metaphorical level, the "*crescendo* principle" was the key to Verdi's entire approach to operatic structure. A musical phrase must *crescendo* in intensity—become more exciting and agitated as it progresses. An aria must *crescendo*—start simply and evolve toward a climax. A scene must *crescendo* and move toward a climax, and an opera must *crescendo* toward its ultimate dramatic denouement.

If the *crescendo* principle is going to dominate the overall shape of a scene or an aria, then it is important to begin, as "De' miei bollenti spiriti" does, in a way that allows room for growth and development. As we have already seen, the scene opens with strings alone, which leaves room for a *crescendo* in instrumentation when the woodwinds and horns enter later. When the singer enters, he too leaves room for growth, beginning with unaccompanied recitative on the words "Lunge da lei per me non v'ha diletto!" ("Far from her, there is no pleasure in life"). After he reflects on this for two brief measures, the entrance of the orchestra and the return to the opening tempo spur Alfredo back into action. (He puts down his gun.)

EXAMPLE 2

[continued]

EXAMPLE 2 [continued]

Keeping the *crescendo* principle in mind, because the overall scene begins with the orchestra alone, followed by unaccompanied voice alternating with orchestral interjections, it makes the moment when orchestra and voice finally join together special. The words "Volaron già tre lune" ("It's already been three months") describe the time the two lovers have spent together, and the first sustained chord in the strings beautifully joins the voice on the word *lune* (months) as this exquisite new texture—voice plus sustained chord—perfectly conveys the sense of how wonderful those three months have been. As is so often the case with great opera composers, the chord on its own is ordinary. The text on its own is ordinary. It is the combination that is magical.

Arioso

Alfredo then goes on to describe all of the things Violetta gave up when she left the social world of Paris to live with him in the country—abundance, love affairs, and pompous parties at which she was the center of everyone's attention. (Notice the character-filled "pompous" rhythm on "pompose feste.") All of this description and all of Alfredo's music in the scene so far has been recitative—free, speech-like vocal writing without rhythmic accompaniment. This creates the opportunity for a next level of expression that is halfway between recitative and real song, called "arioso" (measure 25). This kind of texture, in which the voice and accompaniment begin to have a more regular rhythm and melody but still not the rhythm and melody of real song, is an important element in Verdi's expressive arsenal. Each new texture creates the possibility of a new kind of expression. We are gradually entering Alfredo's emotional world, layer by layer. First we had his casual thoughts expressed in recitative, now in lyrical expression. This new arioso texture allows both the orchestra and Alfredo to paint a beautiful, Norman Rockwell–like picture of contentment that perfectly matches the words "Ed or contenta in questi a meni luoghi" ("Now she is happy in this charming place"). However, a quick harmony change (measure 27) captures Alfredo's brief moment of self-satisfied vanity—"tutto scorda per me" ("she forgets everything for me").

EXAMPLE 3

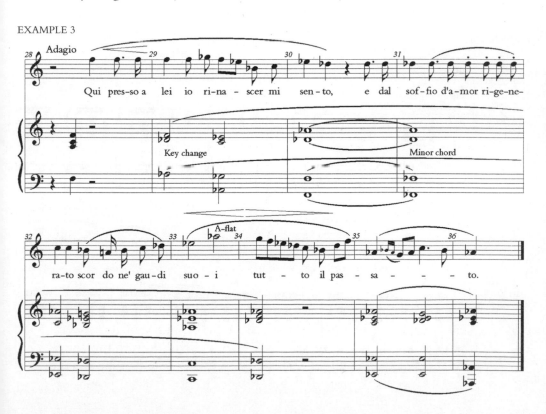

Verdi's sensitivity to the different kinds of expression offered by different musical textures is extraordinary. Up to this point, the piece has had no sustained vocal writing. All of Alfredo's notes have been relatively short and speechlike. However, to describe his bliss—"Qui presso a lei io rinascer mi sento" ("Here near to her I am reborn")—we suddenly get long, expressive, sustained notes and a shift to a new key. Alfredo is literally reborn into a new kind of singing and a new key. The new vocal texture and new key are character developments, not purely musical events. Music and drama are one.

Once the scene has reached this new level of expressive intensity, every image receives heightened musical/emotional treatment. Notice the exquisite minor chord (measure 31) that sets the reference to Violetta's "soffio d'amor" ("breath of love") and starts a *crescendo* to the section's climax. As Alfredo sings of his rejuvenation, he floats up to the longest and highest notes of the entire recitative (measure 33)—a powerful yet simple way for Verdi to complete his carefully constructed *crescendo*. Alfredo has been reborn through his relationship with Violetta, and that rebirth has been beautifully captured by

EXAMPLE 4

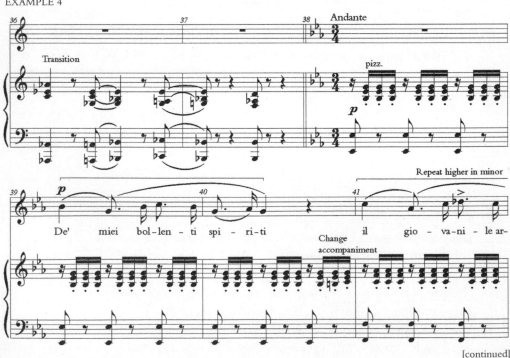

[continued]

EXAMPLE 4 [continued]

the scene's journey from orchestra alone, to voice alone, to vocal recitative, to arioso melody. The next layer of expression will be the aria itself, but first a two-measure transition must find the aria's key—the musical and psychological place from which Alfredo can begin to fully open his heart and sing.

Aria

Like so many Verdi arias, "De' miei bollenti spiriti" begins with the simplest possible "oom-pah-pah-pah, oom-pah-pah-pah" accompaniment imaginable, creating ample room for the aria's upcoming *crescendo* of expression. In a sense, the beginning of a Verdi aria is like the beginning of a chess match. The first few opening moves are "standard" until each game veers from convention and becomes unique. The aria's opening accompaniment figure (measure 38) is fundamentally boilerplate, nineteenth-century Italian opera, though the *pizzicato* violin and viola parts are somewhat unusual and effectively convey the dynamic energy of Alfredo's "bollenti spiriti" ("fervent or passionate spirits"). At first we sense his ardor in small details like the two tiny vocal decorations on "len" of "bollenti" and "ri" of "spiriti," and in the change in the accompaniment on the last beat of measure 40, which urgently pushes the music forward. But Alfredo's impetuosity and passionate spirit quickly start to infect every musical detail. The opening two-measure melody is immediately repeated more urgently—higher and in a minor key (measures 41 through 42). Then the *crescendo* principle takes over, and everything starts to happen faster. As Alfredo's pulse and expression quicken, the accompaniment starts to have more chords per measure and the orchestration thickens. The melody rises higher and higher, and gets louder and louder, until it reaches the phrase's highest note (a G) and climaxes on the phrase's key words—"sorriso dell'amor" ("smile of love"). Violetta has tempered him with her "smile of love," and the five quick notes that soften to a *pianississimo* whisper on "sorriso del-l'amor" ("a perfect representation of that tempering") are as exquisite musically as they are expressive dramatically.

B Section

One of Verdi's greatest gifts was his ability to make an emotional, dramatic point with only a few seconds of music. The entire opening section of this aria is just nine measures long, and the whole middle section is only four measures long, yet in just four measures—approximately fifteen seconds of music—Verdi creates a living, breathing human being.

EXAMPLE 5

[continued]

EXAMPLE 5 [continued]

In this passage, Alfredo is looking back on the day when Violetta said, "Vivere, io voglio a te fedel" ("I want to live faithful to you alone"). Right on the word *vivere*, when he starts to quote Violetta, the music begins to move into a different key, as if to go back in time. This vision of the past lasts for only a moment, however, and the music immediately returns to the home key (measure 51)—to the present—for Alfredo's reaction. This reaction sums up their whole relationship, and it forms the climax of the entire aria. It is the culmination of a dramatic *crescendo* that began with the scene's first note, and it is a superb example of the kind of moment that makes Verdi great. Alfredo is saying that from the moment when Violetta said she would be his alone, the universe was forgotten, and he lives as if in heaven ("dell'universo immemore io vivo quasi in ciel"). Right on the word *vivo* (I live), Verdi rises to a *forte* A-flat, the highest note in the entire aria, as the orchestra plays the most beautiful, heartrending chord in the piece. Everything has led to this one glorious moment. It is the climax of the scene's *crescendo*, which began with orchestra alone and then moved through recitative, arioso, and a first climax on "sorriso del amor" to this final climax on "vivo." This climactic note is not simply a moment of vocal display—an opportunity for a tenor to show off his superb high notes. It is a moment of emotional ecstasy. An opportunity to express through the power of music the inexpressible bliss that love can produce. Music and drama are one. Craft and emotion are effortlessly merged.

EXAMPLE 6

The ending of the aria completes the scene's journey in a wonderful way. The text closes with an image of utter contentment and ecstasy—"io vivo quasi in ciel" ("I live as if in heaven"). Though Alfredo does not know it yet, this blissful existence is about to end, and underneath the vocal line the basses and cellos descend ominously, hinting at the trouble to come (measure 63 and measure 65). The aria ends with Alfredo, amazed at his good fortune, singing over and over to himself without accompaniment, "io vivo quasi in ciel." During this meditation, he pauses on two high notes—an A-flat and a G, the two earlier climaxes of the piece from "sorriso dell'amor" and "vivo"—and with superb craft and symmetry, Verdi resolves these two notes back home to end the piece. For one brief moment, all is well in the world, and this vision of bliss is made all the more poignant by our knowledge that within moments it will be irreparably destroyed as the opera begins its inexorable *crescendo* toward its tragic conclusion.

Truth and Fiction

Though there are several arias in *La Traviata* that are more famous than this one, I have chosen to discuss "De' miei bollenti spiriti" because it illustrates many of the basic musical and dramatic principles at the heart of Verdi's approach to opera in an extremely focused way. However, in addition to all of these principles, there is something else at work in *La Traviata* that is perhaps equally important to an understanding of Verdi's emotional power. As I mentioned earlier, the story of *La Traviata* filters reality through multiple lenses—first Dumas's, then Piave's, then Verdi's—and this filtering ultimately transforms the real Marie Duplessis into Verdi's romanticized Violetta. Similarly, in *Otello*, Verdi and his librettist Arrigo Boito took Shakespeare and added storms, Ave Marias, and other scenes of their own invention until they arrived at an *Otello* that was as "fictional" as *La Traviata*. What is fascinating is that Verdi brought this fictionalizing impulse not only to his operas but to his own life story as well.

When he was sixty-six years old, Verdi wrote a remarkable autobiographical document that that was supposedly published to correct all of the incorrect historical accounts of his youth. The document reads like an opera libretto and describes the tragic deaths of his children and his wife, his depression, his renunciation of composition, and various other significant biographical events. As with *La Traviata* and *Otello*, many of the events did actually occur; however, nearly all of the facts are inaccurate. He has the order of his own children's deaths wrong, and the time frame is completely off the mark. The chronology of his depression is wildly inaccurate, as are innumerable other details. But—and I believe this is the key to the power of Verdi's operas—the document represents the truth *as he felt it*, not *as it actually was*. It was not important to Verdi that he portray Violetta "accurately." What he was interested in was using her as a means of getting at the kind of extreme emotions that we all might feel though rarely get to fully experience or act out. Like Verdi, we all invent the stories of our lives, which often are more about how we wished events to have been (both positively and negatively) than how they actually were. Though these stories may be factually inaccurate, they are emotionally accurate, and they can be as revealing of who we are as the facts themselves.

This is the realm in which Verdi's operas live and breathe. Not the realm of how things really are, but rather the realm of how, if we strip away all of our modern sophistication and cynicism, we wish they could be. These operas speak to the naive part of us that yearns for a partner with whom life would be "quasi in ciel"—as if in heaven. That yearns for a wife as pure and forgiving as Verdi's Desdemona. That yearns for a passionate Verdian world set to exquisite, singable melodies. His operas speak and sing the language of our deepest unspoken wishes, dreams, and fantasies, and in that realm, emotional truth, not factual accuracy, is all that matters.

[14]

Giacomo Puccini
(1858–1924)
"Un Bel Di" from *Madama Butterfly*

─────────

*Massenet feels it as a Frenchman, with powder and minuets.
I shall feel it as an Italian, with desperate passion.*

—GIACOMO PUCCINI

From Verdi to Puccini

Though they spoke different musical languages, Puccini was undoubtedly Verdi's successor in the world of Italian opera. If Verdi was the most significant Italian composer of the second half of the nineteenth century, Puccini was clearly the most significant Italian composer of the late nineteenth century to the early twentieth century. Like Verdi, he was enormously successful during his lifetime, and his works are still at the center of the world's operatic repertoire. Like Verdi, he was single-minded, with opera as his lifelong focus, and like Verdi, he had an uncanny theatrical instinct and a God-given melodic gift that has rarely been equaled. Yet perhaps the most profound connection between the two composers lies in their shared sense of the fundamental source and purpose of opera.

I mentioned the extraordinary fictionalization at the heart of Verdi's operas—his willingness to distort reality in the search for emotional truth—and Puccini's operas were animated by a similar impulse. On any kind of factual, documentary level, an opera like *Madama Butterfly* is utterly absurd. Though Puccini does use several authentic Japanese tunes, and he makes a marginal attempt to get some details of atmosphere correct, no one would ever confuse the opera with a Discovery Channel program on turn-of-the-century Japan. On any realistic level, it is hard to imagine a more preposterous idea than having a Japanese geisha girl sing a love duet with an American naval lieutenant in Italian! However, Puccini, like Verdi, was not interested in historical realism but rather in the reality of our deepest emotions—our wishes, fears, hopes, and fantasies. His goal was not to document the everyday reality of ordinary life, but rather to convey the profoundly human reality of our emotional lives. The power of Puccini's operas begins with their emotional source, and it was at the level of pure emotion that Puccini's decision to compose *Madama Butterfly* began.

Madame Butterfly

In the summer of 1900, Puccini saw David Belasco's one-act play *Madame Butterfly*, based on a story written by the American author John Luther Long. Long's story, which first appeared in *The Century Magazine* in 1898, was based on a real incident related to him by his sister—the wife of a missionary stationed in Nagasaki—in which a Japanese geisha married an American naval officer who then left her for an American bride. Belasco turned Long's story into a one-act play and in March 1900 presented it in New York, where it became an instant success. That same year, Puccini was in London to supervise a performance of *Tosca*, and he happened to see a production of Belasco's play. Although he did not understand a word of English and was unable to follow a single line of dialogue, he was so moved by the essence of the play that he immediately decided to set it to music.

Like *La Traviata*, the opera *Madama Butterfly* takes a story based on real-world events and passes it through multiple filters—John Long's, David Belasco's, Luigi Illica and Giuseppe Giacosa's (Puccini's librettists), and finally Puccini's. In the opera, the basic story involves an arranged marriage between B. F. Pinkerton, a lieutenant in the U.S. Navy, and Cio-Cio San (known as Madama Butterfly), a fifteen-year-old Japanese girl. By Japanese law, the groom is free to dissolve a marriage whenever he wishes, and though Pinkerton is clearly fascinated by his child bride, he in no way sees the marriage as a long-term commitment. Butterfly, however, takes the marriage extremely seriously, and it is this complete difference in their worldviews that leads inexorably to tragedy.

The opera's most famous aria, "Un bel di" ("One Lovely Day"), takes place near the beginning of Act II, after Pinkerton has been gone for three years. Though this aria is often excerpted from the opera as a whole, the music of the preceding scene is crucial to its full impact. The second act opens with an extended conversation between Butterfly and her faithful maid Suzuki in which we learn that with Pinkerton gone, Butterfly's financial situation is precarious. When Suzuki tells Butterfly that no foreign husband has ever returned home to his Japanese bride, Butterfly becomes furious and says, "He'll return." Suzuki, faithful maid that she is, says, "Let's hope so."

EXAMPLE 1

[continued]

EXAMPLE 1 [continued]

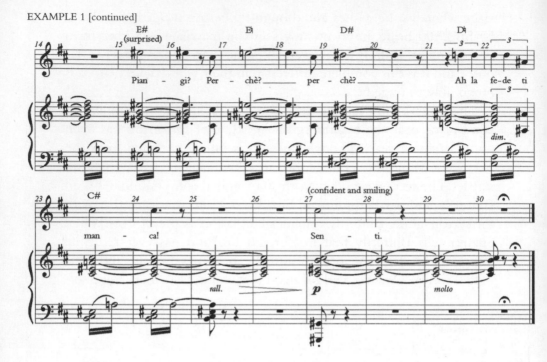

As Butterfly tries to convince both Suzuki and herself that Pinkerton will come back, the music perfectly captures the psychological anxiety and turbulent emotions surrounding the scene.

Dissonant harmony and urgent tremolos create the anxious atmosphere of the exchange. Butterfly conveys her certainty that Pinkerton will return by singing "Tornerà" ("He'll return") on a single note, and Suzuki expresses her acquiescence by singing "Speriam" (Let's hope so) on the same note. Butterfly's insistence that Suzuki repeat the words with her is perfectly depicted by the music's insistently moving a step higher for her second "tornerà." But Suzuki is now too overwrought to simply repeat Butterfly's music on a single note, and instead her vocal line leaps up in anguish. As the orchestra matches her passion with a *forte* outburst, Suzuki bursts into tears. Then, in a perfect melding of music, text, and emotion, as Butterfly asks Suzuki why she is crying, she tries to calm both herself and Suzuki down by moving down a scale in half steps—E#–E–D#–D–C#. By the time she has reached the word "Senti" ("Listen"), she has completed a journey from anxiety to belief. She has transitioned musically to the key in which she will sing her aria, and she has transitioned psychologically to the emotional place from which she can begin to sing.

EXAMPLE 2

The contrast between the turbulence of the Suzuki-Butterfly exchange and the simplicity of the beginning of the aria could not be more striking. After the gradual descent to a C♯ on "Senti," the aria's opening high G-flat seems to float in from another world—*da lontano* (from far away). (This effect is completely lost in excerpted perform-ances that begin with this note.) There is not a single note outside of the home key—not a single accidental—in Butterfly's entire first phrase. She is sure of her vision—"Un bel di, vedremo levarsi un fil di fumo sull'estremo confin del mare. E poi la nave appare" ("One lovely day we'll see a thread of smoke rise at the farthest edge of the sea, and then the ship will appear"). However, though she has faith, she sings softly. At this point in the aria's journey, her faith is as much hope as it is belief, and the beautiful, major-key cadence at the end of the phrase perfectly captures her joy as she sees Pinkerton's ship appear in her mind's eye. The music "arrives" (cadences) as Pinkerton "arrives" in her imagination.

EXAMPLE 3

As the aria progresses, Butterfly begins to fully inhabit her vision, causing the scene to unfold with increasing urgency. "Poi la nave bianca entra nel porto, romba il suo saluto. Vedi? E venuto" ("Then the white ship enters the port and thunders a salute. You see? He's come"). The music moves into a minor key, and the tempo gets faster (*un poco mosso*). (Notice the ship's cannon thundering its greeting in the orchestra in measure 13.) The four-measure phrase of measures 9 through 12 is copied higher in measures 13 through 16, creating more emotional urgency as Butterfly sees Pinkerton's arrival. As she vividly lives out every emotion of this imaginary scene, her childlike coyness is heartbreaking. "Io non gli scendo incontro. Io no." ("I don't go to meet him. Not I"). With exquisite emotional and musical subtlety, the harmony changes "sweetly" ("*dolcemente*") on the second note of measure 17, showing us the exact moment when Butterfly shyly decides not to run and greet Pinkerton.

EXAMPLE 4

As with so many great opera composers, some of Puccini's most powerful dramatic effects are also his simplest. To convey the image of Butterfly waiting and waiting—"Mi metto là sul ciglio del colle e aspetto, e aspetto gran tempo" ("I shall wait there on the brow of the hill and wait, and wait a long time")—Puccini simply rocks back and forth monotonously between the same two chords ("chord 1" and "chord 2") over and over again.

EXAMPLE 5

[continued]

EXAMPLE 5 [continued]

Every detail of the unfolding scene is painted from Butterfly's emotional point of view. As she imagines Pinkerton emerging from the city's crowd ("E uscito dalla folla cittadina"), a syncopated rhythm in the woodwind accompaniment—Butterfly's heartbeat—sharply contrasts the static "waiting chords" of the preceding phrase and makes the moment come to life. Puccini again brings out Butterfly's childlike side as she wittily and lovingly describes Pinkerton as a "little dot"

("un picciol punto"), followed by orchestral unisons and a slower tempo that perfectly capture the image of Pinkerton starting slowly up the hill ("s'avvia per la collina"). Butterfly's distracted vocal rhythm (with a wonderful muted-trumpet accompaniment) is a perfect equivalent to her psychological state as she wonders, "Who will it be?" and "What will he say?" ("Chi sarà? Chi sarà? E come sarà giunto che dirà? Che dirà?") Then, in a moment that almost defines Puccini, we suddenly feel the heartbreaking power of memory and recollection. As Butterfly imagines Pinkerton calling her name from the distance ("Chiamerà Butterfly dalla lontana"), the orchestra plays the music of memory—their exquisite love music from Act I—and this poignant reminder of the past is emotionally devastating.

The conclusion of the aria is opera at its most powerfully dramatic. Puccini returns to the music that began the aria, but now Butterfly sings at full volume, *fortissimo, con molto passione* (with much passion). This reprise is not simply louder, it is an affirmation of her faith as she tries to salvage a belief in her future.

EXAMPLE 6

[continued]

EXAMPLE 6 [continued]

The major-key cadence in measure 56 radiantly concludes Butterfly's imaginary reconciliation with Pinkerton, followed by a single minor chord that jolts her out of her reverie (measure 57). In the brief, overwhelming coda that follows, Butterfly reenters reality, shifts her focus to Suzuki, and insists that everything she has described will happen. "Tutto questo avverra, te lo prometto. Tienti la tua paura, io con sicura fede l'aspetto." ("All this will happen. I promise you. Keep your fears, I with firm faith will wait for him"). The phrase builds in volume, climbs higher and higher in pitch, and concludes with a shattering *fortissimo* final high note (the highest note of the aria) filled with every extreme emotion a human being could possibly feel—hope, fear, desperation, worry, conviction, and finally belief. This extraordinary note is a product of Butterfly's entire life experience. Though she began the opera as a child, through her journey of love, pain, and disappointment, she has defiantly become a woman of strength. The aria ends with Butterfly and Suzuki embracing, not so much as mistress and maid but as women sharing their suffering, while the orchestra plays a wordless, conciliatory version of the aria's opening phrase. The phrase's closing cadence was initially a cadence of hope (measure 8). Then a cadence of belief (measure 56). Now heard for the third time (measure 69), it is a cadence that acknowledges in the orchestra what can never be. It is now a cadence of acceptance.

Puccini Then and Now

It has become commonplace today to criticize *Madama Butterfly* for its racist, imperialistic, stereotypical portrayal of Asian individuals, and for its trivialization of Japan's culture and customs. Without attempting to deny the validity of these criticisms, there are two important points to be made. First of all, though we may choose to express our interest and enthusiasm for Japan and its cultural traditions in a different, more "authentic" way today, it was this same enthusiasm for things Japanese that motivated Puccini. When Japan opened its doors to the West in 1854 after two hundred years of isolation, the entire European art world was affected, and Puccini was one of a large group of composers who eagerly explored the new sound possibilities suggested by Oriental scales, rhythms, and instruments. Puccini actually met with the celebrated Japanese actress Sadayakko to get a sense of "the high twitter" of a Japanese woman's voice, and he asked the wife of the Japanese ambassador to procure sheet music from Japan and to sing native songs for him to write down. He expanded his percussion section in an attempt to imitate some of the exotic sounds he heard from Japanese musicians, and though none of these percussion instruments or Japanese songs were used "authentically" as they might be today, given the context of his time, there was nothing racist or condescending about Puccini's approach.

In the end, however, *Madama Butterfly*'s Japanese surface was not and is not the key to the opera's power. Puccini was ultimately no more interested in authentically depicting an actual Japanese geisha than Verdi was in depicting an actual Parisian courtesan. Puccini called *Madama Butterfly* a "*tragedia giapponese*"—a Japanese tragedy—but in fact it was not a Japanese tragedy but a human tragedy, and that is the key to its effectiveness. Puccini, like Verdi, had the courage to believe that the core human passions are deeper than our differences of language and customs. That people's needs, wants, desires, and sufferings are universal, and can be expressed movingly and convincingly in any authentic musical language. That the pain of betrayal transcends culture, and that beyond our many differences, on some basic, fundamental level, we are all the same. *Madama Butterfly* does not deny difference, it attempts to transcend it, and it is on this universal, human level that the work succeeds or fails. *Madama Butterfly* speaks directly from the heart in the hope that other hearts will respond, and whatever Puccini might have gotten wrong, the worldwide love affair the work has created for over a hundred years shows that he got what was essential right.

[15]

Johannes Brahms
(1833–1897)

A-Major Intermezzo,
Op. 118, No. 2

You must gradually learn to know all the most important works of all the important masters. The study of the history of music and the hearing of masterworks of different epochs will speediest of all cure you of vanity and self-adoration.

—ROBERT SCHUMANN,
MAXIMS FOR YOUNG MUSICIANS

The Classical Romantic?

Today we take the importance of an historical perspective for granted. If you're a painter, you study the paintings of the Great Masters; if you're a philosopher, you study Plato and Aristotle; and if you're a musician, you study the music of Bach and his predecessors. However, in the nineteenth century, this kind of historical perspective was radically new. Until then, composers and listeners were almost completely uninterested in music written before their time. New music was all that mattered, and old music was at best a curiosity. For the

Romantics, however, history mattered, and no nineteenth-century composer was more obsessed with the past than Brahms. As Brahms's biographer Jan Swafford points out, Brahms owned a valuable collection of musical manuscripts and autographs and was intensely involved with the newly emerging discipline of historical musicology. As artistic director of the *Gesellschaft der Musikfreunde* in Vienna, he single-handedly extended the concert repertoire backward to the Baroque and beyond, and he was largely responsible for tilting the balance in performance in favor of old music rather than new music. As a composer, Brahms was so overwhelmed by the legacy of Beethoven that he was unable to bring himself to write a symphony until he was forty-three, and it is no coincidence that his first three symphonies were popularly called Beethoven's Tenth, Brahms's *Pastoral* Symphony, and Brahms's *Eroica*. He was obsessed with his place in history, and he was deeply worried that his music would fade into oblivion because it was neither avant-garde nor progressive.

At the heart of the famous Brahms-Wagner controversy that divided the European musical world during the last third of the nineteenth century was a fundamental disagreement over the role of history. To the radicals in the Wagner-Liszt camp, the future of music lay in rejecting the past in favor of new forms and new modes of expression, while Brahms and his conservative supporters believed profoundly in the value of tradition. Though Brahms was thrust into this debate unwillingly and actually had great respect for Wagner's music, there is no doubt that the two composers approached the past in fundamentally different ways. At the age of twenty-seven, Brahms wrote in his notebook, "Form is the product of thousands of years of the greatest masters' efforts and is something that each new generation cannot assimilate too quickly. It is but the delusion of misguided originality to seek in one's own limited universe to achieve a perfection that already exists."

Brahms's belief in the value of the past and the importance of tradition influenced every aspect of his music. In an almost direct repudiation of Wagner's enormous operas and the sprawling tone poems for huge orchestras that were fashionable at the time, Brahms choose to compose symphonies and concertos for Classical-sized orchestras in Classical forms, as well as chamber music and solo works that followed directly in Beethoven's footsteps. Brahms was obsessed with traditional counterpoint—canons, fugues, and the like—and his entire approach to form, compositional technique, and orchestration was deeply conservative. He defiantly insisted on writing absolute music without any specific program—music that would rely solely on its own inner logic and expressive powers. His craft-oriented credo comes out clearly in his advice to a fellow composer, "Work at it over and over again, until . . . there is not a note too many or too little, not a bar you could improve on. Whether it's beautiful too is an entirely different matter, but *perfect it must be*." This emphasis on perfection before beauty, craft before expression, and unassailable compositional logic led many critics and historians to label Brahms "the Classical Romantic"; however, his music was actually far more complex than this simple label might imply.

In one of the most perceptive observations ever made about Brahms, the philosopher Friedrich Nietzsche said, "If we discount what he imitates, what he borrows from great old or exotic modern styles . . . what remains as specifically his is yearning." Not perfection, not craft, not unassailable logic, but yearning. In spite of his legendary personal reserve, guardedness, uncommunicativeness, and secrecy, Brahms's music is music of deeply felt emotion, yet emotion that is always held in check by a superbly accomplished, carefully constructed technique. It is as if the music's yearning is always pushing against its technical reserve, and this push and pull of emotion and technique— the desire to say more (for intimate communication) while not wanting to say too much—is at the core of the music's power.

The Golden Years

In the summer of 1890 Brahms was fifty-seven years old. He'd had enough of composition, and decided to call it quits: "I've been tormenting myself for a long time with all kinds of things, a symphony, chamber music and other stuff and nothing will come of it. . . . I'm just not going to do it anymore." However, within a year of "quitting," he had finished the G-Major String Quintet, the Clarinet Trio, and the Clarinet Quintet. To continue his "retirement," he then wrote twenty piano pieces from 1892 to 1893—op. 116 to 119. Jan Swafford's biography of Brahms describes the six pieces of op. 118 as "scientific studies of compositional craft disguised as pretty little salon pieces," and at first glance they seem to be a throwback to the past. Short intermezzi, ballades, and romances—piano miniatures—were new and progressive when Schumann wrote them in the 1830s, but sixty years later they were almost reactionary, and the forms of these pieces are as conservative as the genre. All six numbers in op. 118 are clear, three-part ABA forms that are easy to grasp on first hearing. Yet the music within these seemingly conventional forms is profoundly moving, profoundly individual, and far more radical than it might first appear.

The A-Major Intermezzo is the second piece in the op. 118 set. Without any introduction whatsoever, the opening piece immediately plunges the listener into its turbulent, almost improvisatory-sounding emotional universe.

EXAMPLE 1

The piece makes no attempt to ease the listener into its intense, compositionally dense style, and Brahms has to struggle to wrestle its relentless, swirling energy into submission in order to end the work. Though the music seems to be heading for a minor-key ending, as if by magic, the final three measures shift to major, and the piece dissolves in a long, slow, major-key arpeggio beginning with the lowest note of the piano.

EXAMPLE 2

This final A-major chord is both an ending to the first piece and a preparation for the second, which begins with the same A-major chord; however, the relationship between the two pieces goes deeper than a single shared chord. The opening piece's complexity, turbulence, and struggle are what Brahms must work through in order to arrive at the lyrical song of the second piece. It is as if for Brahms to speak directly from the heart, he must first labor to get there. Brahms wrote to Clara Schumann, "Have I not often told you how seldom I succeed in getting my thoughts out of my heart and onto paper? It is exactly the same with my composing. It simply won't flow from my heart." Speaking from the heart may have been challenging for Brahms compositionally and personally, but it is the struggle to do so that makes the opening phrase of the A-Major Intermezzo so poignant.

EXAMPLE 3

Heart and Mind: Phrase 1

Though on first hearing this opening phrase sounds like a simple, beautiful, spontaneous melody, nothing is ever as simple as it seems in Brahms's music. Even his most lyrical melodies tend to be made out of tiny, developable motives. For reference, I will call the two key gestures of this opening, "1 2 up" and "1 2 leap" (see score). Though we will not realize it until the remarkable climax of the piece, the melody of "1 2 up," really wants to resolve down, like this:

EXAMPLE 4

However, Brahms raises the last note an octave higher, turning the gesture into an exquisite leap—"1 2 leap"—with a roll in the right hand (measure 2) to emphasize the leap.

The possibilities that Brahms hears in these two tiny three-note gestures are astonishing. After a short continuation, the two gestures return to begin the second half of the phrase, but now they are subtly and beautifully reharmonized.

EXAMPLE 5A   EXAMPLE 5B

After the phrase finally cadences at measure 8 (see example 3), the entire opening repeats *pianissimo*, as if Brahms had revealed too much and now needed to whisper.

A Step Forward/A Step Backward: Phrase 2

This quintessentially Brahmsian sense of opening one's heart only to immediately step back and retreat underlines the next phrase as well. After a yearning three-note idea is stated once (notice the characteristic *crescendo-diminuendo*; a step forward, then a step back), then repeated more urgently, it flowers into what feels like an emotional, six-note confession (measures 16 through 20). The whole unit ("yearn-yearn-confess") is then repeated higher and *crescendos* as the "confession" is achingly extended to seven notes (Nietzchean "yearning"), only to again fall back and trail away (measures 20 through 24).

Brahms unfolds his emotional world slowly, with great discretion, one step at a time.

EXAMPLE 6

What happens next is a classic example of how Brahms's superb compositional technique can transform a seemingly conventional moment into something original and fresh. One of the standard, form-defining events in a piece of classical music is the return of an opening theme, and the next five measures of the piece (measures 25 through 29) are a masterful preparation for the return of the piece's opening gesture—"1 2 up, 1 2 leap." As the melody *crescendos* and climbs up a simple scale, the phrase's "new" idea—"**1 2** up, short, long" (see score)—begins to hint at the piece's opening three notes. The idea is immediately repeated higher, and then seems to begin a third statement, but before we know it, the phrase climaxes, the *crescendo* reaches *forte*, and somehow we find ourselves back at the "leap" of "1 2 leap!"

EXAMPLE 7

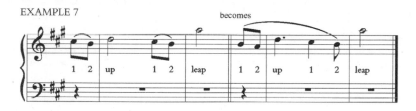

Looking back at this wonderful moment shows us the kind of technique that makes Brahms great. As you can see in example 7, in order to smoothly elide the return to the opening idea, Brahms lowers two notes of "1 2 up" and rhythmically varies "1 2 leap," so that it is only when we reach "leap"—the rolled chord of measure 30—that we realize we are in fact back at the opening idea. A simple return now sounds fresh and surprising. Crafting unexpected seams and connections like this is one of the ways Brahms is able to give new life to traditional forms, and not realizing that we are back at an opening idea until that idea is already under way is one of Brahms's favorite compositional devices and is found not only in his piano pieces but in his symphonies and chamber music as well.

EXAMPLE 8

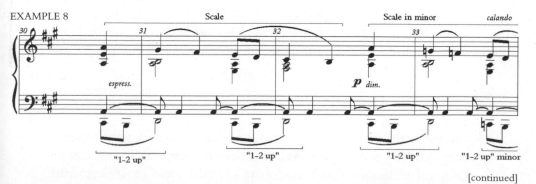

[continued]

EXAMPLE 8 [continued]

Now that we have returned to the intermezzo's opening idea, Brahms's unique mixture of heart and mind begins to show itself in all its glory. While the right hand plays a new, lovely, descending scale, the left hand takes the opening three notes of the piece—"1 2 up"—and repeats them over and over again down low as an accompaniment. Then, as the right hand hauntingly shifts the new scale into a minor key (measures 33 and 34), "1 2 up" shifts exquisitely to minor as well. (**C♯**–B–D becomes C♮–B–D.) The moment is both technically ingenious and exquisitely poignant. Heart and mind are one.

Brahms the Radical: Phrase 3

The revolutionary creator of the twelve-tone system, Arnold Schoenberg, went to great lengths to depict Brahms as a radical with a compositional technique that Schoenberg claimed was a precursor to his own. The key idea was Brahms's innovative use of what Schoenberg called "developing variation": basing an entire composition on a small musical cell that continuously evolves and develops itself. At heart, "1 2 up," one of these small cells, is barely a musical idea at all. Yet this tiny musical molecule has not only generated the intermezzo's opening melody but also transformed itself into a repeating accompaniment that shifts keys from major to minor. And that is only the beginning. Though the passionate melody that follows sounds completely new (measures 34 through 36), it is in fact "1 2 up, 1 2 leap" turned upside down, or inverted! (Inverting a musical idea, as we saw in chapter 2, turns each ascending interval into a descending interval and vice versa.)

So often Brahms's most beautiful, spontaneous-sounding melodies are also his most cerebrally constructed, and the ending of the A section is an extraordinary example of this kind of fusion of intellect and emotion. Because this section will eventually return to finish the intermezzo, these measures must ultimately resolve the entire piece, and they do so in a way that is as remarkable as it is simple. The piece began with "1 2 up, 1 2 leap" (see example 9). To end the A section, Brahms puts "1 2 up" an octave lower in the middle of the right hand, and then does both "1 2 leap" and its resolution ("1 2 down") at the same time! The higher A in the right hand is the original "leap," and the lower A is the long-sought resolution. Never has music that seemed to sing this simply been so cerebrally constructed. Never have emotion and intellect combined more effortlessly or more beautifully.

EXAMPLE 9

EXAMPLE 10

The B Section

The middle section of this intermezzo (measures 49 through 76) is a classic example of the kinds of fresh possibilities Brahms is able to find hidden beneath seemingly conventional, conservative surfaces. The opening of the section immediately creates the kind of contrast we expect in the middle of a traditional ABA piece. The key shifts to minor, the rhythm shifts to triplets, and the writing becomes more

contrapuntal. The entire section is all based on one, seemingly brand–
new musical idea stated in the section's opening four measures—
essentially a descending scale in the right hand echoed (for four notes)
by the left hand.

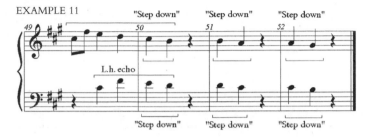

EXAMPLE 11

The second phrase (measures 57 through 64, example 10) shifts the
theme to a major key, changes the texture to choralelike chords, and
compresses the idea to its first five notes (C♯–F♯–E♯–D♯–C♯), then just
four (F♯–E♯–D♯–C♯) done as a round between the two hands (see
score). Suddenly the material has a completely different mood and
feel, as if we are penetrating beneath its surging surface to a more con-
templative, profound, hushed core. But as is so often the case with
Brahms, as if he has revealed "too much," he immediately pulls back,
and the third phrase returns to the key and setup of the first phrase
while reversing the role of the two voices: the lower voice now leads
and the upper voice follows.

EXAMPLE 12

[continued]

EXAMPLE 12 [continued]

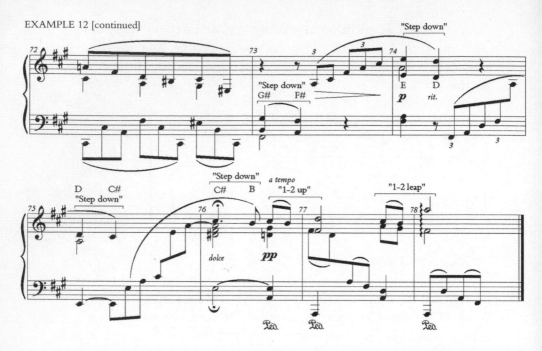

As beautiful as these three phrases are, it is the magical transition back to the opening music (measures 73 through 76) that really shows Brahms's greatness. As you can see in example 11, embedded in the main idea of this section is a tiny, two-note fragment, which I have labeled "step down." It has been a part of all of the material of the section so far, but now Brahms drops everything to focus on this fragment. The third phrase finishes with "step down" on the notes G#–F# (measure 73). The next measure does it a step lower on E–D, and then still another step lower on D–C#. Then, in a stunning moment, measure 76 continues the pattern still one step lower, to C#–B, and we suddenly discover, to our amazement, that these two notes are the first two notes of "1 2 up"—C#–B–D! To make sure we do not miss what is happening, there is a fermata to call attention to the moment, and the two notes, C# and B, are played twice—once stretched out rhythmically, and then once in the original tempo so the connection will be clear. Suddenly the A and B sections of the piece, which had previously seemed unrelated, have been connected by a tiny, motivic molecule—"step down." An almost clichéd formal moment—the return of the A section in a traditional ABA form—has been given new life, beauty, meaning, and expressivity by the sheer force of Brahms's technique and imagination.

To Make the Past Bear Fruit

One of the reasons that Brahms's music is so popular today is that, in a sense, it allows us to have our cake and eat it too. We get to experience the harmonic richness and emotional intensity of late-Romantic music expressed with Classical-period clarity, rigor, and logic. Brahms's music satisfies both the heart and the mind while blending the old and the new in a uniquely fresh way. It has become commonplace today to think of Brahms as a lone, solitary figure—the great conservative of the late-Romantic era—without followers or influence in the twentieth century. Someone who created a unique, unrepeatable synthesis of classical forms and romantic content through the strength of his own personal, artistic will. And if we think of Brahms's compositional legacy as symphonies, concertos, chamber music, and solo music in classical forms with Romantic content, then it is largely true that the twentieth century did not pursue this path. But if we think of Brahms's legacy in a larger sense as the powerful belief that who we are today in the present can grow meaningfully out of engagement with the craft, tradition, and wisdom of the past, then Brahms's impact has been substantial and can be seen in a wide variety of twentieth-century composers who mixed their own contemporary musical language with traditional forms and techniques, like Ravel, Shostakovich, Prokofiev, Barber, Britten, and Bernstein.

Brahms believed that if we deeply immerse ourselves in the past and bring the world of the present to bear on this material, a new, creative synthesis can emerge. Perhaps part of his legacy is the belief that the past is a prison only if our knowledge of it is superficial—if we imitate it rather than integrate it with the present. Revering and admiring the past does not inevitably lead to copying it. As Stravinsky said so beautifully in *Poetics of Music,* "Tradition is a living force that animates and informs the present. Far from implying the repetition of what has been, tradition . . . appears as an heirloom, a heritage that one receives on condition of making it bear fruit before passing it on to one's descendants."

Brahms inherited a tradition, made that tradition bear fruit, and passed it on, and long after many more "fashionable" composers have faded from memory, it is Brahms's music that survives. It has become part of our tradition and our heritage, and it continues to be a "living force" that "animates and informs" our musical present.

[16]

Antonín Dvořák
(1841–1904)

Slavonic Dance, Op. 46, No. 8

---

*It must be something respectable for I don't want to let
Brahms down.*

—ANTONÍN DVOŘÁK

An Extraordinary Friendship

Sometimes you can judge an artist's talent not simply by the work he
creates, but by the kind of respect and loyalty he generates in other
artists, and there is no more striking example of this than the relationship between Brahms and Dvořák. In 1874, Brahms was world
famous, living in Vienna, the musical capital of Europe, while Dvořák
was a starving, unknown composer from Bohemia. That year, Brahms
sat on the jury dispensing the Austrian State Stipendium, and he was
so overwhelmed with the music Dvořák submitted that he awarded
him enough money to enable him to survive and focus on composition. Brahms then asked his own publisher, Fritz Simrock of Berlin,
to publish Dvořák's music, which almost instantly made Dvořák both
rich and famous. Brahms also prevailed upon an influential editor to
write a major article about Dvořák, and when Dvořák went to America, Brahms offered to copyedit and proofread Dvořák's music for

him. Finally, believing that no composer from Bohemia could possibly be a success without coming to live in a cultural capital like Vienna, he offered to fund Dvořák's relocation. The fact that Dvořák refused, remaining Czech both geographically and musically, was crucial to his success, as he was able to create something utterly fresh and new by blending Brahms's world of conservative, Germanic compositional craft with his own Bohemian, folk-music world.

The op. 46 *Slavonic Dances* for piano four hands was the work that launched Dvořák's career, and it was both published and commissioned by Brahms's publisher, Fritz Simrock. The title of the work not only reflects Dvořák's compositional and political ambitions, it also shows Simrock's astute understanding of the contemporary classical-music scene in Europe. For Dvořák, writing the *Slavonic Dances* was a political statement; a reaction against the overwhelming dominance of Austria in Europe's political and cultural landscape. Dvořák's dances are purposefully *not* Austrian dances—waltzes, minuets, or *Ländler*—but Slavonic dances modeled on the dances of Poland, Ukraine, Serbia, and elsewhere. Writing the *Slavonic Dances* was part of Dvořák's lifelong struggle to establish the legitimacy of the Czech language and culture. He spent years battling to have his publisher print his name as "Antonín" rather than the German form, "Anton," and to have the titles of his pieces printed in Czech as well as German in his scores.

Dvořák's nationalistic fervor was, of course, part of a much wider European phenomenon, and the evolution of national musical styles, country by country, was a central development of the second half of the nineteenth century. The enormous success of Brahms's *Hungarian Dances*, published by Simrock in 1860, had already shown the public's enthusiasm for fundamentally Viennese music flavored with piquant nationalistic touches, and the decision to commission the *Slavonic Dances* was clearly a response to Brahms's earlier success. Today, Dvořák's dances are heard almost exclusively in their orchestral versions in concert halls and on recordings; however, in the nineteenth century, four-hand piano music written for amateur music making at home was the route to commercial success, and it was the original piano-duet version of the *Slavonic Dances* that brought Dvořák and Simrock fame and fortune.

One of Dvořák's greatest gifts as a composer was his ability to write effectively for instrumentalists of widely varying levels of ability. Though the *Slavonic Dances* surely benefit from performance by gifted professional pianists, they can also be played successfully by amateur pianists, and both piano parts are challenging enough to be rewarding yet not too difficult so as to be overwhelming. In addition, the frequent repeats of individual phrases and entire sections of music give both listeners and performers multiple opportunities to grasp the piece's elements. If a rhythm, figuration, or ensemble problem trips up the performers the first time through, by the time the passage has returned a third or a fourth time, the technical or musical challenge can usually be overcome. The *Slavonic Dances* were a perfect match for Dvořák's and Simrock's audience, and the music gives us a wonderfully vivid picture of the abilities, needs, and interests of the performers and listeners who made up that audience.

Folk Dances?

Though the *Slavonic Dances* were clearly inspired by Brahms's *Hungarian Dances*, one of the key differences between the two works was their relationship to their source material. Put simply, Brahms's dances were settings of actual folk melodies, while Dvořák's were not. The *Slavonic Dances* were an attempt to capture the spirit of the folk dances of his native Bohemia as well as those of Slovakia, Moravia, Silesia, Serbia, Poland, and Ukraine, but Dvořák created idealized forms of these dances, not transcriptions or arrangements of actual folk material. He filtered these folk-dance forms through his own extremely sophisticated, European compositional language, and his effortless fusion of the serious and the popular begins with the piece's opening phrase.

EXAMPLE 1

[continued]

EXAMPLE 1 [continued]

Both the opening and closing numbers of the op. 46 *Slavonic Dances* (numbers 1 and 8) are *furiants*, which the *Harvard Dictionary of Music* defines as "a rapid and fiery Bohemian dance, in 3/4 time, with frequently shifting accents." One of the characteristic *furiant* rhythms that often results from these "frequently shifting accents" is a pattern called hemiola. Put simply, in three-quarter time, beats are normally grouped in sets of three with an accent at the beginning of each measure—**1**23, **1**23, **1**23, **1**23. However, if the accent is shifted, the music can be momentarily grouped in sets of two—**1**2 **3**1 **2**3 **1**2 **3**1 **2**3. Going back and forth between these two different groupings is called hemiola, and this pattern is familiar to anyone who has ever listened to "America" from Leonard Bernstein's *West Side Story*.

EXAMPLE 2

Hemiola—alternating groups of two and three beats—is the rhythmic key to Dvořák's *furiant*, and it begins with the opening measures. Though the whole phrase (and piece) is written in three-quarter time, the music really shifts back and forth between groups of two and three beats, like this:

EXAMPLE 3

[continued]

EXAMPLE 3 [continued]   Groups of 2   Groups of 3

However, it is not only the hemiola rhythm that makes this opening so catchy and so "Bohemian"; it is also the sudden shift from a minor key in the first four measures to a major key for the second four measures. Rapid alternation of major and minor keys and hemiola rhythms are typical characteristics of *furiants*, yet Dvořák incorporates these folk-like features in an opening phrase that has the classical balance, concision, and symmetry of a Brahmsian scherzo. Once this unique mixture of Slavonic spirit and European technique has been established, Dvořák's compositional craft begins to work its magic in earnest.

Furiants typically contrast intense, loud, "furious" ideas, like Dvořák's opening idea, with softer, more relaxed ideas like the next eight measures (example 1, measures 9 through 16), and on first hearing, the music of this second phrase could not sound like more of a contrast. The dynamic level switches from *fortissimo* to *piano*, the thick chords of measure 1 are replaced by a single-line melody, and the accompaniment in the second piano relaxes into a straightforward oompah-pah, oompah-pah pattern. However, if you listen more closely, you realize that the rhythm of the melody, with the exception of the last measure, is identical to that of the first phrase. (The overall melodic shape is similar as well.) Not only does this rhythm connect what appear to be two contrasting ideas, it also gives the fundamental hemiola idea of the piece a subtle new twist. If you listen to the rhythm of the second piano part throughout this phrase, it is clearly in groups of three—123, 123, 123, et cetera. However, the melody in piano 1 has the hemiola rhythm of the first phrase, which means that measures 9 and 10 and 13 and 14 have different accent patterns in the two piano parts at the same time! The melody is in groups of two while the accompaniment is in groups of three, creating a wonderfully sophisticated, subtle rhythmic tension.

As I mentioned earlier, one of the things that makes this piece so accessible is the way it frequently repeats individual phrases and entire sections of music. Both phrase 1 and phrase 2 are eight measures long and are immediately repeated, so when phrase 1 returns as phrase 3 and is again immediately repeated (example 1, measures 17 through 24), there is not only a satisfying sense of a musical bookend but an expectation that the piece will continue in the same way: with more eight-measure phrases, each immediately repeated. However, instead, Dvořák subtly varies the form and avoids mechanical predictability by writing an eight-measure phrase (measures 25 through 32) that for the first time *does not* repeat.

EXAMPLE 4

[continued]

EXAMPLE 4 [continued]

EXAMPLE 4 [continued]

One of Dvořák's greatest talents was his ability to focus a musical moment so that it "reads" to the listener. His music is "gettable" without being simple. The melody of the next section (measures 41 through 64), for example, is clearly a variation of the opening tune, but the musical highlight of the phrase is actually the exotic chord in the accompaniment in measure 43 and measure 47 (Wagner's "Tristan chord" in a different harmonic context!), and everything is designed to underline this chord. It is the only chord in the passage that is not simply a B-flat chord—it is marked with an accent and a *sforzando*, and Dvořák adds a third voice in the accompaniment to mark each entrance.

We cannot miss the moment, and Dvořák brings this same clarity of focus to the way he handles repetition in the passage. If the piece's "default setting" is to repeat each eight-measure idea *once*, Dvořák subtly varies the structure here by repeating the passage's eight-measure idea *twice*, with each repeat increasing in intensity. The first repeat decorates the melody in the right hand of piano 1 (measures 49 through 56). The second repeat *crescendos*, moves the tune down low into the left hand of piano 2 (measures 57 through 60), and then decorates it in continuous eighth notes to lead to a dramatic return of the opening theme (measure 65, example 5). This return has a brand-new, driving bass line in the accompaniment—again utterly gettable—and the repeat of the opening phrase serves as a powerful bookend to conclude the first large section of the piece.

Transition and Theme 2

The transition to the second theme is a classic example of Dvořák's deceptively effortless technique. As we have just seen, the first section of the piece ends powerfully with a return of the opening theme accompanied by a new, driving bass line. To transition to the second theme, Dvořák simply takes the opening theme's final two measures and repeats them over and over again: first exactly (measures 73 through 76), then slightly simplified (measures 77 through 84). Next, in a spectacular moment that seems both spontaneous and inevitable, these two measures effortlessly become the accompaniment to the piece's second theme.

EXAMPLE 5

[continued]

EXAMPLE 5 [continued]

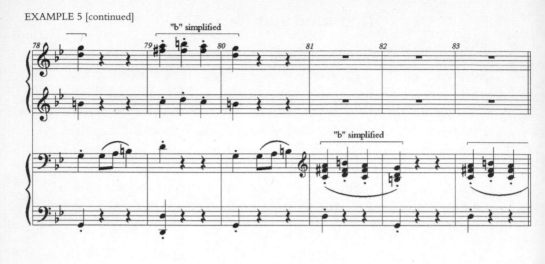

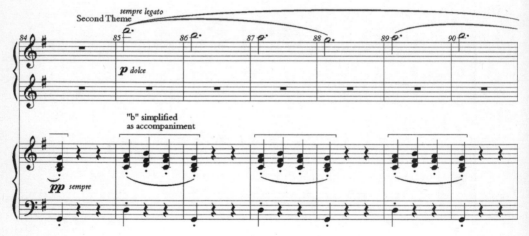

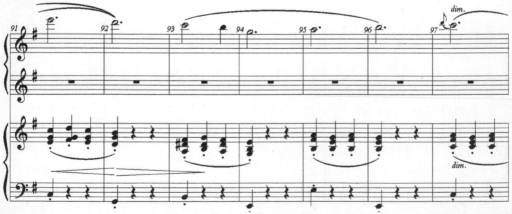

[continued]

EXAMPLE 5 [continued]

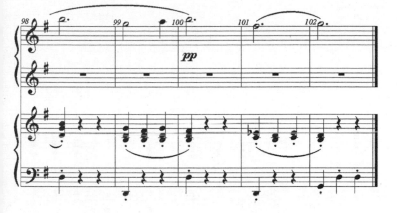

Dvořák's transformation of this fiery, powerful cadence music into a relaxed, easygoing accompaniment is accomplished with such ease that we barely notice the superb technique, and the way the lovely, pastoral second theme that floats above this accompaniment is spun out for a full eighteen measures seems equally effortless. The tune repeats once with easily recognizable folklike decorations, and then fades into the distance, echoing its four-measure ending over and over again in a classic Dvořák *diminuendo*. (If you listen closely, however, you will notice that the harmony is different under every repeat.) Everything seems peaceful and serene until the opening theme returns with a jolt to begin a complete repeat of the opening section.

EXAMPLE 6

[continued]

EXAMPLE 6 [continued]

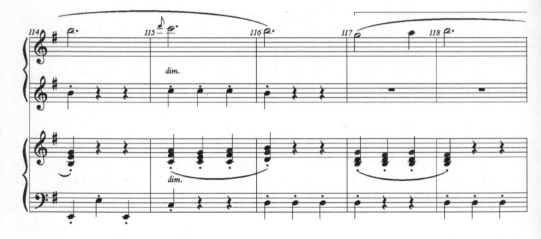

[continued]

EXAMPLE 6 [continued]

Coda

After hearing the entire opening section repeated, we expect a repeat of the transition and second theme as well, but surprisingly, Dvořák skips directly to a coda instead. This coda is a superb fusion of European craft and Bohemian spirit, and it makes a powerful conclusion to the entire op. 46 set. Since he has already used the *last two measures* of the opening theme to make his original transition, with impeccable logic he now uses the *first two measures* of the opening theme ("a") to generate his coda.

EXAMPLE 7

[continued]

EXAMPLE 7 [continued]

An exciting coda that intensifies the musical drama fits perfectly within the folk *furiant* tradition; however, the compositional craft in this section comes right out of Brahms. Dvořák works with his musical ideas as if he were composing a symphony, not a Slavonic dance. He reduces the opening theme to its first two measures and then repeats the fragment three times with increasing intensity, each time higher. (On a G chord, then on an A-flat chord, and then, surprisingly, on a B-major chord.) The ascent finally climaxes on a D, and a more-normal, eight-bar phrase closes the thought. As the passage begins to repeat, we are sure we will hear the whole phrase a second time as we have in the piece's other repeats. However, in a brilliant stroke, instead of climaxing on D, Dvořák, shockingly, goes a step higher, this time to an E (measure 220), moving the music away from the home key! To add insult to injury, he repeats the phrase a second time (measures 224 through 227), but just as we are beginning to panic, he effortlessly slides back to the home key (measures 228 through 231), and all seems well with the world.

Surely at this point, we think, we are only a few measures away from ending, yet Dvořák has one more surprise in store. Instead of simply finishing the piece with a few measures of flourish, he transitions to the piece's lovely second theme—a theme we never expected to hear again. After a surprising repeat of the entire second theme, Dvořák once again echoes its closing measures, softer and softer, and slower and slower, until one final, abrupt statement of the last four measures of the opening theme (without the first four!) powerfully ends the piece. What was originally an opening idea has become a

EXAMPLE 8

[continued]

EXAMPLE 8 [continued]

closing idea, giving the piece a perfectly symmetrical ending that seems like so many of the wonderful passages in this book—both inevitable and surprising at the same time.

Influence vs. Imitation

During his extended visit to America from 1892 to 1895, Dvořák became fascinated with American indigenous music—in particular the music of the American Indians and Negro spirituals. Perhaps the overriding message of his three-year stay in America, articulated frequently in the press, was his belief that America needed to create a school of composition based on its indigenous folk music. Referring to Negro spirituals he said,

> These are the folk songs of America and your composers must turn to them. All the great musicians have borrowed from the songs of the common people. Only in this way can a musician express the true sentiment of his people. He gets into touch with the common humanity of his country.

In a sense, Dvořák was simply projecting his experience with his own indigenous folk music onto the Americans. "The songs of the common people" and the folk material that were the sources of the *Slavonic Dances* were a crucial element in Dvořák's compositional style. They were the way he got "into touch with the common humanity of his country." However, Dvořák, like Chopin, and Tchaikovsky, who also worked with folk material, brought himself, not a blank slate, to these influences. Though biographers might like to paint a portrait of a humble, peasant Dvořák—a man of the people and an apprentice butcher in his teens—he was also an enormously sophisticated musician, up-to-date on all the latest compositional developments. Dvořák became famous when he began to bring all of himself to his music—his rigorous, European compositional technique, and his Bohemian folk-music world. He absorbed the spirit of his folk material—its clarity of expression, simplicity of resources, and rhythmic life—but only its spirit. Which is ultimately the difference between influence and imitation. To be truly open to what someone else or some other culture has to say requires the confidence to step outside your world and look at it or hear it from another point of view. But in the end you must filter what you have seen or heard through your own worldview if you are to produce anything authentic.

In an interview in the *New York Herald*, Dvořák said, "You must not imitate. Model your style upon all that is best, all that is noble and elevated in the literature of music, but remain yourself. Do not become the copyist of anyone, for you will invariably copy your model's defects while his merits will be so subtle that they will escape you." Dvořák listened to everything, learned from everyone, yet proudly remained himself and copied no one. Brahms knew authenticity when he heard it—personally and musically—and he respected it. Dvořák knew he could never be Brahms, but he could be Dvořák. Once he fully embraced that choice, he found his voice. Residence in Vienna was not required.

[17]

Peter Ilich Tchaikovsky (1840–1893)

"Trepak" from
The Nutcracker Suite

I sit down to the piano regularly at nine-o'clock in the morning and Mesdames les Muses have learned to be on time for that rendezvous.

—PETER ILICH TCHAIKOVSKY

A Russian Romantic?

Few composers have been more misunderstood than Tchaikovsky. The tabloid nature of his private life—his lifelong struggle with his homosexuality, his disastrous seven-week marriage followed by a suicide attempt, his bizarre fourteen-year relationship with a benefactress whom he never met, and the still-controversial facts about his death— has often drawn attention away from his disciplined, craftsmanlike approach to composition and has frequently led to major misconceptions about his work. Though to many people Tchaikovsky's music almost defines the term "Russian music," when replying to his fellow composer and student Sergei Taneyev's statement that the only way forward for Russian music was through music with roots in the people, Tchaikovsky said,

> If thanks to Peter the Great, we have been fatefully caught on the tail of Europe, then thus we shall remain forever. I value very highly the wealth of material which the "slovenly and suffering people" [Taneyev's phrase] produce, but we, i.e., we who use this material, will always elaborate it in forms borrowed from Europe—for, born Russians, we are at the same time even far more Europeans, and we have so resolutely and deeply fostered and assimilated their forms that to tear ourselves from them we would have to strain and do violence to ourselves, and from such straining and violence nothing artistic could come.

In fact, Tchaikovsky was not only *not* a Russian-nationalist composer, he had contempt for Russian-nationalist composers like Mussorgsky, Cui, and Borodin, all of whom he considered dilettantes. In spite of his popular image as the quintessential Romantic composer—pure emotion, melody, and instinct—Tchaikovsky was actually the most technically trained Russian composer of the nineteenth century. He was a professor of composition for twelve years at the Moscow Conservatory and the author of the very first textbook on harmony in Russian, *Guide to the Practical Study of Harmony*. Like Dvořák and Brahms, he had a superb compositional technique capable of absorbing nearly any kind of ethnic influence within his European-based language, and there is no better example of this than his famous *Nutcracker Suite*.

The Nutcracker Suite (1892): The Art of Orchestration

If Schubert can be said to have single-handedly taken a minor genre—art song—and turned it into a vehicle for significant compositional expression, then Tchaikovsky did essentially the same thing for ballet music. Before Tchaikovsky, almost no one took ballet music seriously. It was largely decorative, almost always of poor quality, and completely lacking in compositional prestige. Tchaikovsky's three great ballets, *Swan Lake*, *The Sleeping Beauty*, and *The Nutcracker*, completely revolutionized the art of composing for the dance and transformed ballet music into an essential dramatic component of the form and a significant musical genre worthy of the attention and efforts of the greatest composers.

Today the ballet *The Nutcracker*, adapted from E. T. A. Hoffman's fairy tale *The Nutcracker and the Mouse King*, is probably the most widely performed ballet in the world; however, it was the music—in particular the music of the suite, first performed as a sneak preview for the complete ballet—that initially was successful with the public. The ballet itself was largely a failure, and it took many years for it to gain a foothold in the ballet repertory. *The Nutcracker Suite* contains very little of the music that actually carries the ballet's plot forward but instead focuses almost exclusively on the second-act dances that take place in the Kingdom of the Sweets—"Dance of the Sugar Plum Fairy," "Trepak" ("Russian Dance"), "Coffee" ("Arabian Dance"), "Tea" ("Chinese Dance"), "Dance of the Mirlitons," and "Waltz of the Flowers." One of the keys to Tchaikovsky's greatness as a ballet composer, evident in all of these famous *Nutcracker* dances, was his ability to instantly capture the essence of a scene, a character, or a mood in a single musical idea, and it is often his brilliantly theatrical orchestration of these ideas as much as their notes, rhythms, and harmonies that makes them so effective. For example, the entire world of the Sugar Plum Fairy is instantly conjured up by the sound of the celesta—a brand-new instrument patented in 1886 that Tchaikovsky had just discovered and desperately wished to keep secret until the *Nutcracker* premiere.

EXAMPLE 1

Similarly, the Chinese world of "Tea" is instantly brought to life by Tchaikovsky's brilliantly eccentric orchestration, in which two *staccato* bassoons chortle in their lowest registers accompanying a

EXAMPLE 2

solo flute in its highest register with no other instruments in between.

In both of these examples, orchestration is not just "window dressing" but rather an essential, expressive component of the musical idea, and the same thing is true in "Trepak." Though "Trepak" is frequently subtitled "Russian Dance," the Trepak or Tropak is actually a traditional Ukrainian folk dance from the Slobozhan region of Ukraine. The dance, often performed on celebratory occasions, is usually in quick two-four time in a major key. The harmony tends to be extremely simple, and the tempo gradually speeds up throughout the dance. Like Dvořák, Tchaikovsky modeled his piece on an ethnic folk dance without quoting actual folk material, and like Dvořák, Tchaikovsky used all of the resources of a sophisticated European composer to create a stylized, "artified" version of an authentic ethnic dance. However, unlike Dvořák, Tchaikovsky had no nationalistic political agenda behind the piece. "Trepak" was simply one of a series of colorful, theatrical, "national" dances in *The Nutcracker*, and it was no more significant to Tchaikovsky than the Chinese dance or the Arabian dance that occurred in the same scene.

Like so many of the dances in the *Nutcracker*, "Trepak" sounds simpler than it actually is. Here is a clumsy "Kapilow version" of the opening eight-measure idea that keeps Tchaikovsky's melody but changes the accompaniment:

EXAMPLE 3

Here is Tchaikovsky's version:

EXAMPLE 4

Notice that my version begins with a boring, regular, accompaniment that has a chord on every beat. Two chords per measure (Bum Bum / Bum Bum / Bum Bum / Bum Bum). Tchaikovsky, however, begins the piece with an orchestral jolt—a single, *forte* chord—then unaccompanied first violins followed by three fast, exciting chords (measure 2) that drive powerfully to the third beat (Bum rest / Bum bum bum / Bum rest / Bum bum bum). The orchestration beautifully punctuates this pattern with brilliant, *forte* orchestra chords on the downbeat of measures 1 and 3 and thin orchestration in between. In addition, if you listen closely to the difference between the simple, folklike chords that I wrote in measures 2 and 4 and the sophisticated ones Tchaikovsky wrote, you will begin to hear the European technique hidden behind the folk façade.

One of the things that made Tchaikovsky such a superb ballet composer was his theatrical feeling for narrative flow—his ability to create a musical plot that continually moves forward—and the melody beautifully complements both the accompaniment and the orchestration. Without the two fast, decorating notes in the first measure, the theme would simply begin with four uninteresting repeated notes (G, G, G, G, not G, G, **F♯**, G, G). However, these two fast notes give life and character to the figure and turn it into the key motive of the entire piece ("x" in example 4). Measure 2 completes the idea, and Tchaikovsky immediately repeats the combination lower in measures 3 and 4 to cement it in the listener's ear. Like the syncopated accompaniment, the melody of the second half of the phrase (measures 5 through 8) effectively contrasts the first half, and a powerful "bum bum bum" cadence brings the opening phrase to a striking close. Though this opening *antecedent phrase** races by in about five seconds, it is the key to the entire piece. It instantly grabs the attention of the listener and creates the world of "Trepak" in a single, memorable idea. In classic Tchaikovsky fashion, the three fast notes at the end of the phrase (measure 8) lead explosively back to a repeat of the opening idea, and an altered ending closes the thought (measure 16).

I mentioned that Tchaikovsky was a superb orchestrator, but great orchestration is not simply a matter of arranging the notes of a piece well for instruments but rather of using orchestration as an integral tool to help shape and structure the dramatic flow of a piece. Since the overall form of "Trepak" is basically AABA, we get to hear this opening phrase (A) three times; however, each successive version is orchestrated more and more brilliantly. The second version adds brass and percussion to the opening chord, changes the dynamic marking from *forte* to *fortissimo*, adds woodwinds to thicken the first-violin melody to two octaves, adds instruments to the "bum bum bum," and gives a whole new color to the syncopated accompaniment by adding tambourine and timpani. (The timpanist plays two notes at the same time, which was relatively unusual at this point in music history.) Every detail of this repeat is reorchestrated to increase the excitement and intensity, and even the three fast notes that lead back to the opening gesture are now expanded from three instruments to seven instruments and from a single octave to three octaves.

Contrast: The B Section

The middle section of the dance (measures 33 through 57) contains the only contrasting music in the piece, and though at first hearing the material sounds completely new, it in fact is all subtly derived from the piece's opening measure.

EXAMPLE 5

The melody is now on the bottom of the orchestra (lower strings, bassoons, and bass clarinet) with the accompaniment above, but though the texture and tune are new, the core of the melody—its first four notes—is still "x" (see score). Tchaikovsky immediately copies this "new" idea (xvar) lower to reinforce it (measures 35 and 36), but if you listen closely you can also hear the same idea echoed in the woodwinds in measures 34 through 36. This kind of sophisticated development and overlapping of musical ideas has absolutely nothing to do with Ukrainian folk dances but everything to do with Tchaikovsky's refined, European compositional technique. However, Tchaikovsky's technique is so accomplished, you barely notice the effortless way the second half of the idea speeds up the dramatic action (measures 37 through 40) by using the first three notes of "x" to rise excitedly up the scale higher and higher, followed by a brilliant flourish in the lower strings to thrillingly finish off the thought. Though all of this material sounds exciting and new, it is all subtly and beautifully derived from the opening measure of the dance!

Tchaikovsky's brilliant orchestration contributes enormously to the excitement of this passage as well. A standard orchestration of the accompaniment would simply have both first and second violins playing repeated chords, like this:

EXAMPLE 6

Instead, Tchaikovsky has the first and second violins alternate every beat, which gives enormous energy to the passage, particularly when the chords begin to change faster in measure 36.

EXAMPLE 7

Similarly, a normal orchestration would have the three flutes play the simple repeated chords of example 6. Instead, the flutes constantly switch octaves, and their leaps add a unique energy to the passage. Tchaikovsky isn't simply orchestrating the notes of the dance; he is orchestrating its excitement.

EXAMPLE 8

Because the form of the piece up to this point has been so square—sixteen measures A, sixteen measures repeat of A, sixteen measures B—the eight extra measures that Tchaikovsky adds to prepare for the return to the opening music (measures 49 through 56) make an enormous impact.

EXAMPLE 9

Once again, the material initially sounds strikingly new. Until this moment, the piece has really contained no chords outside of the home key, and the striking appearance of a *fortissimo* brass-and-woodwind C-minor chord (measure 49) creates a new sense of urgency and drama. We know that something important is about to happen.

Suddenly, the basic eight-measure musical unit of the piece shortens to two measures, then one measure, then half a measure in length, and we realize that we are at the dramatic center of the piece: its moment of greatest tension. Yet once again, the musical material is all derived from the opening idea, now reduced to its three-note essence (x). This essence repeats over and over again on three different notes until with an extraordinary sense of release. the opening section returns for its third and final appearance (measure 57).

Return and Coda

Like the superb craftsman he was, Tchaikovsky has carefully saved his most brilliant orchestration of this opening section for last. For the first time, the tambourine strikingly doubles the rhythm of the opening melody—now played by all of the violins and all three flutes—while the dynamic level remains *fortissimo* throughout. This and many other small orchestral changes combine to make this final statement of the tune the most thrilling of all the versions. Yet after repeating fifteen of the section's sixteen measures, Tchaikovsky still has one more trick up his sleeve—a dazzling sixteen-measure coda.

Everything combines in this brilliant coda to create the kind of inten-

EXAMPLE 10

[continued]

EXAMPLE 10 [continued]

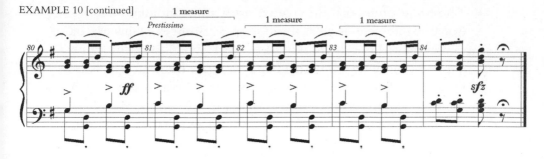

sity and over-the-top excitement that almost defines Tchaikovsky's music. Like a tightening screw, the musical units dramatically get shorter and shorter as four-measure phrases (measures 69 through 76) shorten to two-measure phrases (measures 77 through 80) and finally to one-measure phrases (measures 81 through 83) to drive to the close. At the same time, the tempo is speeding up, the music is getting louder, and new orchestral devices—a brand-new tambourine and trumpet rhythm, thickening brass parts, and a final tambourine trill—continue to propel the music forward to an electrifying close. When the piece ends, it is hard to know who is more exhausted and exhilarated: the dancers, the orchestra, the conductor, or the audience. In a little over a minute of music, Tchaikovsky has masterfully conjured up the world of a Russian folk dance as seen through the eyes of a sophisticated, European composer: utterly inaccurate, utterly inauthentic, yet utterly thrilling.

A "Child of Glass"

When Tchaikovsky was a young boy, his nurse, Fanny Durbach, said he was "a child of glass"—"un enfant de verre"—and his intensely emotional reaction to events would continue throughout his adult years as well. As a Christian, he was tormented by being homosexual, and his life was filled with shame, repression, and the fear that his "sickness" would be discovered and brought out into the open. Music was the only realm in which he could safely express the full intensity of his emotions, and it was the only realm in which these emotions could in some sense be controlled and disciplined. The near-hysterical intensity of so much of Tchaikovsky's greatest music clearly has its source somewhere in his personal life, yet, as he himself points out, the relationship is anything but straightforward. In a letter to his patroness, Nadezhda von Meck, he wrote:

Those who think that the creative artist at the moment of emotional excitement is able, through the resources of his art, to express what he feels are mistaken. . . . Having no reason to be happy, I can fill myself with a happy creative humour and, conversely, in a happy situation produce a piece that is imbued with the most gloomy and hopeless feelings. In a word, the artist lives a double life: that common to mankind, and that of the artist, and sometimes, moreover, these two lives are not congruous. However this may be, I repeat that, for composition, the most important condition is the possibility of separating oneself, if only for a while, from the cares of the first of these two lives, and devoting oneself exclusively to the second.

Perhaps no artist lived a more poignant "double life" than Tchaikovsky: the torturous, uncontrollable, emotionally intense life "common to mankind," and the disciplined, conscientious, controlled life of art. Yet in spite of the remarkable control he was able to exert over his art through his prodigious compositional technique, he was also acutely aware of the importance of what he poetically referred to as "that supernatural, incomprehensible force which no one has explained and which is called inspiration." Tchaikovsky's music lives or dies on the strength of themes that often seem to be the product of pure inspiration. Melodies like the horn theme of the Fifth Symphony's second movement, the second theme of the "Elegie" from the *Serenade for Strings*, and the second theme of the Sixth Symphony seem to be compositional gifts-from-the-Gods, arriving, as Tchaikovsky put it, "not through searching but of their own accord." It may have been craft and technique that enabled him to develop these inspired ideas to nearly unbearable, almost-hysterical levels of emotional intensity, but no composer has been granted a purer melodic gift or a more seemingly unending supply of inspired themes and melodies than Tchaikovsky.

In a powerful moment of self-awareness Tchaikovsky wrote, "Laziness is a very powerful human trait. For an artist there is nothing worse than to give way to this. You cannot simply wait. Inspiration is a guest who does not like visiting those who are lazy. She reveals herself to those who invite her. You must, you have to overcome yourself." And that is the truly poignant aspect of Tchaikovsky's biography. It is the story of a perpetual depressive, tortured and unhappy throughout nearly his entire life, who "overcame" himself over and over again, and through tireless self-discipline, self-criticism, revision,

prodigious effort, and study managed to produce one of the most significant bodies of music of the nineteenth century. In an unbearably
sad quotation, Tchaikovsky summed up his life: "Regretting the past,
hoping for the future, and never being satisfied with the present—
there is the story of my life." Yet fortunately, there was also the story
of his art: the music that overcomes it all.

[18]

Claude Debussy (1862–1918)

"Des Pas sur la Neige" from *Preludes*, Book I

Works of art make rules; rules do not make works of art.

—CLAUDE DEBUSSY

"Make It Mine; Make It New"

If any kind of continuing thread can be said to run through the twentieth century's bewildering variety of musical languages and styles, it is an impulse that might be summed up by the phrase "Make it mine; make it new." This compulsion on the part of twentieth-century composers to make each piece completely individual, with its own personalized musical language—and to never repeat the past, either their own or someone else's—is evident in the work of nearly all of the century's major composers, and it continues as an underlying aesthetic today. However, though the rhetoric of the century may have been dominated by talk of leaving dead traditions behind, in fact, the new has always been created as a response to the old, and for many twentieth-century composers, Debussy, consciously or unconsciously, was where the century meaningfully began.

Debussy the Impressionist?

Perhaps the single word used most frequently to describe Debussy's music is "Impressionist," and it is almost impossible to find a CD or score of his music that does not have an Impressionist painting on the cover. The original connotation of the term was highly negative, and Debussy despised being called an Impressionist; however, in spite of his lifelong protests, his name has been inextricably linked with the word since 1887, when his youthful exam piece, *Printemps*, received this critique in a report of the secretary of the Academy of Fine Arts:

> M. Debussy certainly cannot be blamed on the score of either platitude or banality. He has, on the contrary, a marked—perhaps too marked—tendency to cultivate the strange and the unusual. He clearly has a strong feeling for colour in music which, when exaggerated, causes him to forget the importance of clarity in design and form. It is very much to be hoped that he will be on his guard against that vague *"impressionism" which is one of the most dangerous enemies of truth* [my italics] in any work of art.

Without entering into the hundred-year-old debate over whether Debussy was or was not an Impressionist, there is no doubt that there were elements of his aesthetic that in some sense overlapped with the Impressionists and perhaps even more powerfully with the Symbolists. If Impressionism has frequently been described as an attempt to suggest rather than to depict, to portray not an object but an emotional reaction to an object, or to capture fleeting impressions rather than permanent realities, it is hard not to feel a similar spirit when Debussy in an interview said:

> I confess that I live only in my surroundings and in myself. I can conceive of no greater pleasure than sitting in my chair at this desk and looking at the walls around me day by day and night after night. In these pictures I do not see what you see; in the trees outside of my window I neither see nor hear what you do. I live in a world of imagination, which is set in motion by something suggested by my intimate surroundings rather than by outside influences, which distract me and give me nothing.

The central credo of the Impressionists and Symbolists, "Pas la couleur, rien que la nuance!" ("No color, nothing but shades!"), could be Debussy's credo as well, and it is a perfect description of his spell-binding prelude "Des Pas sur la neige" ("Footsteps in the Snow").

A Prelude to What?

Debussy wrote his first book of twelve preludes in only two months, between December 1909 and February 1910, and he later wrote a second book of twelve preludes, published in 1913. The idea of writing twenty-four preludes clearly came from the twenty-four preludes in each volume of Bach's *Well-Tempered Clavier*, yet in *The Well-Tempered Clavier* each prelude was "functional": it was a prelude to the fugue that followed. Debussy's preludes, however, like Chopin's, are quintessentially romantic. They are preludes to nonexistent continuations. Preludes to nothing but other preludes. Today, pianists frequently perform and record one or both of the two books of preludes as complete units; however, this was never Debussy's intention. He assumed that each prelude was sufficiently self-contained to be performed either as an individual piece, or as part of a small group of preludes, and though "Footsteps in the Snow" is only thirty-six measures long, its hypnotic, self-referential world contains the seeds of a quietly understated revolution whose effects are still being felt today.

EXAMPLE 1

Debussy draws us into the piece's subtle, nuanced universe before a single note has been played. In the original versions of the *Preludes*, the titles do not appear at the beginning of the pieces at all, but only at the end of each prelude, as if they were afterthoughts (which in fact they were). To emphasize this "afterthoughtedness," Debussy puts each title in parentheses, poetically preceded by three dots: (. . . Footsteps in the Snow). In addition, he adds a beautifully evocative performance direction below the first measure, "This rhythm must have the sonorous value of a melancholy and frozen landscape." Once the piece begins, Debussy's subtle dynamic markings further enhance the refined atmosphere. The prelude speaks in a whisper with a dynamic range that extends only from *pianississimo* to *piano*—from incredibly soft to soft. Remembering the Symbolist credo, "Pas la couleur, rien que la nuance!" ("No color, nothing but shades!"), this is music that revels in nuances and shades and lives or dies on the ability of a sensitive listener to respond to its exquisite subtleties.

The Opening Phrase

If you listen closely to the notes of the opening phrase, you will notice that there are actually two different voices in the left hand. First, there is what I will call the "footsteps motive" (D–E, E–F), which is a distinctly separate voice from the repeated D's underneath. (Notice the beautiful blur created when the second note of each footstep sounds against the repeated D's.) There are actually two footsteps, a left foot (D–E) and a right foot (E–F) if you will. I said that this piece was quietly revolutionary, and part of its quiet revolution is its quiet obsession—its "footsteps fixation." Twenty-five of the prelude's thirty-six measures contain these two identical, snowbound footsteps. Always the same notes. Left foot, right foot. D–E, E–F.

The variety of shades and colors that Debussy is able to find in these two simple footsteps is astonishing. In the first phrase, the left hand repeats the paired footsteps (plus D's) four times. Above this, the right hand adds a third level to the texture: a classic Debussy non-melodic "melody" that begins by elegantly fitting into the rhythmic pauses in the footsteps and, after a delicate overlap, finally forms a complete, three-note D-minor chord to close the phrase at the end of measure 4. Debussy's unique approach to melody had a major impact on the music of many twentieth-century composers. A well-known story tells of a Viennese banquet during which an official tried to compliment Debussy by suggesting that his musical experiments had "abolished melody." Deeply offended, Debussy acidly replied, "But my dear sir, my music aims at nothing but melody." All his life, Debussy was accused of abolishing melody. Critics complained that his operas didn't sing and that no one could whistle his tunes, yet in the evocative, spare atmosphere of "Footsteps in the Snow," the simple, restrained, nonmelodic "melody" of measures 2 through 4 (example 1) is as "expressive and painful" (Debussy's marking) as any traditional melody. Debussy didn't abolish melody, he reinvented it.

EXAMPLE 2

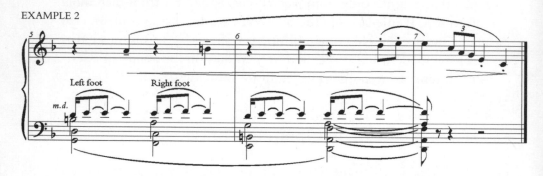

Phrase 2: The Art of Reharmonization

What happens next is a classic example of the power of Debussy's subtle art. The piece's "footsteps fixation" continues with two more pairs of footsteps (measures 5 and 6). However, in a complete contrast to the spare, ascetic opening version, Debussy now puts four exquisitely rich chords underneath the footsteps in a previously untouched, low register of the keyboard (each chord progressively lower and richer harmonically), giving the two familiar footsteps a breathtaking new sound. It is the austerity of the first phrase that makes the second phrase sound so lush in contrast, and as the right hand climbs up a simple scale, getting louder and louder (though still within an incredibly soft overall dynamic level), and higher and higher, the left hand descends lower and lower, and the combination produces the kind of subtle, restrained climax that is a hallmark of Debussy's style.

The technical term for repeating a single note or a short musical idea while changing the accompanying harmony is reharmonization, and reharmonization plays an enormously important role not only in this prelude but in nearly all of Debussy's music. Reharmonizing a melody is a kind of musical equivalent to Monet's painting the same cathedral or haystack at different times of day in different light, and reharmonizing the prelude's footsteps and placing them in subtly different musical contexts is the primary compositional work of this piece. That an idea as simple as these two footsteps could generate such an emotionally rich and varied prelude is the miracle of "Footsteps in the Snow," and Debussy proves himself to be as masterful as Bach at creating the "whole from a single kernel."

EXAMPLE 3

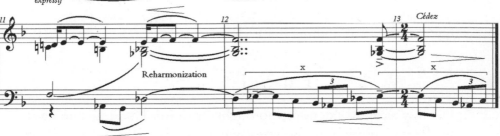

Phrase 3: Dissonance

The sound world of the prelude's first phrase was spare and austere. The second phrase was marked by a shift to richly expressive harmony. The third phrase again changes expressive worlds and dramatically discovers dissonance and a new kind of anxious, intense, chromatic harmony. Though the melody of this phrase is simply four more sets of footsteps, the accompanying chords come from a completely new harmonic universe. For Debussy, the introduction of this new sound world is a major event. In addition, the piece begins to develop rhythmic motion with two bass notes for each set of footsteps, and we begin to get a hint of an actual melodic line in the lowest voice.

Pieces like "Footsteps in the Snow" teach us to listen for the subtleties and nuances in music and in life that normally pass by unnoticed. Because Debussy focuses so obsessively on his footsteps melody, tiny details have a disproportionally large impact. Measure 9, for example, is an exact repeat of measure 8 except that the last note in the left hand is an octave higher. Then, just as that small change is registering, measure 10 eliminates the left hand on the first beat, creating a wonderful, momentary sense of space as if the bottom has suddenly dropped out—but only for a single beat. Finally, due to the virtually identical, basic harmony of measures 8 through 10, the subtle reharmonization of the footsteps in measure 11 is exquisitely expressive and powerful enough in this relatively static context to create a cadence that brings the thought to a close.

However, in a stunning, though subtly stunning, moment, Debussy now puts aside his footsteps fixation for the first time. While the right hand sustains a single chord for eight beats, the left hand exults in its freedom by playing a short, melodic fragment that has nothing to do with the footsteps ("x"). Though by any traditional standards this little fragment hardly qualifies as a melody, in this spare, footsteps-dominated universe, it sounds incredibly melodic. ("But my dear sir, my music aims at nothing but melody.")

Frozen Footsteps

Debussy received extensive, thoroughly traditional musical training at the Paris Conservatoire and was a winner of its most prestigious composition prize, the Prix de Rome; however, he was deeply skeptical of the entire academic approach to composition. He abhorred the whole Germanic concept of development and form and constantly strove to find new ways of developing musical ideas and structuring a piece of music. He was a great admirer of Mussorgsky's, and in a Debussy review of one of the Russian composer's song cycles we get a sense of what Debussy was striving for in his own music. Mussorgsky's music, he said, "resembles the art of an enquiring savage discovering music step-by-step through his emotions, no particular form or rather, one so varied as to be completely unrelated to anything systematic or academic, since it depends on and is made up of successive minute touches mysteriously linked together by the gift of an instinctive clairvoyance." Mussorgsky aside, this is almost a perfect description of the form of "Footsteps in the Snow," which is itself "unrelated to anything systematic or academic," and is made up of ever-new harmonizations of the opening footsteps "mysteriously linked together by the gift of an instinctive clairvoyance."

EXAMPLE 4

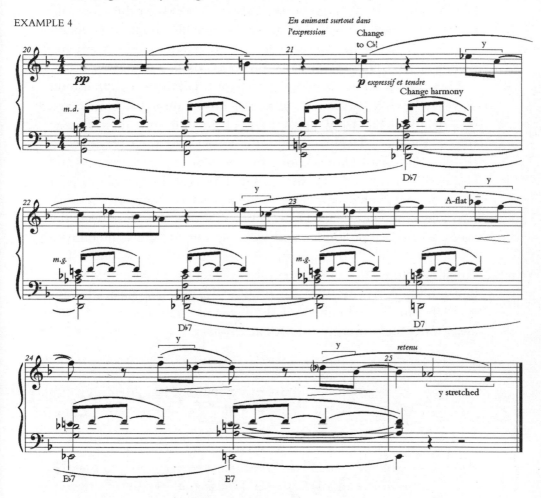

Debussy despised the traditional sonata-form approach to structure, and its labels and categories rarely apply to his music. For example, when the prelude eventually returns, after several more footsteps reharmonizations, to the music of the four exquisite chords (see measure 5, example 2), this return functions nothing like a recapitulation in a sonata or a return in any other traditional musical form. It lasts for only one measure, and its purpose is solely to create an expectation in the listener that can immediately and expressively be violated. Put simply, when we hear the music of measure 5 in measure 20, we expect to hear the music of measure 6 in measure 21. However, a slight change in the melody (C-flat, not C-natural) leads to a beautiful and completely unexpected chord in measure 21 that is sustained for eight beats (for musicians, a D-flat dominant-seventh chord as opposed to the earlier D-minor chord). Though the difference between the chords in measure 6 and measure 21 is subtle (listen carefully to both examples), in Debussy's world this kind of difference is a major event, and this surprising chord begins the push to the piece's understated climax.

Up to this point in the prelude, we have heard thirty-two footsteps, and they have always come in pairs. A left foot immediately followed by a right foot. Suddenly, the left foot becomes frozen, and for the first time in the piece, Debussy insistently repeats only the right footstep (E–F) seven times! The harmony becomes more intense as well and begins to rise upward (measure 23) in a kind of floating chord progression that would influence a great deal of twentieth-century harmony (for musicians—Db7–D7–Eb7–E7). At the same time, the music is also getting louder, and Debussy says to "above all animate the expression" ("en animant surtout dans l'expression"). The "melody" climbs to a two-note sigh ("y") on the highest note of the piece so far (A-flat, measure 23), but immediately falls back, after this typically understated climax, as the two-note sigh repeats and fades away, lower and lower, and slower and slower.

EXAMPLE 5

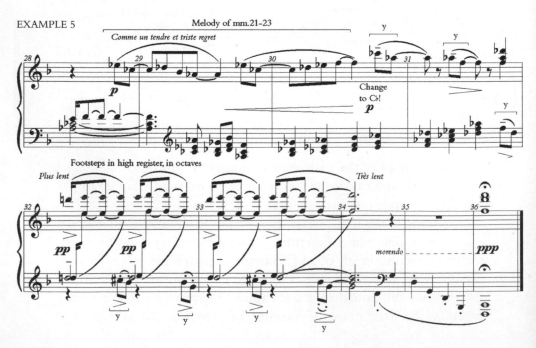

Transcendence: Conclusion

This prelude is in no traditional form, yet in its own unique way, the entire piece has beautifully set the stage for its magical ending. As we just saw, the melody that rose to a subtle climax in measure 23 was still "imprisoned," so to speak, by the frozen-footsteps accompaniment. Four measures later, however, Debussy brings back the same melody and liberates it. Instead of playing footsteps in the accompaniment, the left hand is set free. Simple chords rise higher and higher, and in the context of the prelude's constricted universe, this ascent creates an enormous effect. The melody of example 5 copies the melody of example 4, but the climax reaches delicately higher this time—not to A-flat, but to C-flat, the new highest note of the piece (measure 30, beat 3). One measure later, we are on the verge of a real cadence. The sun has come out and melted the frozen landscape. There is hope amid the desolation. But instead of moving into a traditional cadence, in a subtly shocking moment, the chord resolves completely unexpectedly back to the original footsteps, but now, for the only time in the piece, the footsteps are in octaves and a full octave higher than any previous statement (measure 32).

The notes of these final footsteps are the highest notes of the entire prelude. Debussy, with characteristic restraint, has saved this register of the piano for this one magical moment, and after two final pairs of footsteps, the prelude doesn't really end but simply finishes by falling into the only stable home chord of the entire piece (D minor). Though the chord is fundamentally a traditional chord, its spacing makes it sound almost surreal. It contains both the lowest and highest notes of the entire prelude, with a huge gap in between the hands, and it is marked *ppp*—*pianississimo*. With a subtlety that almost defines Debussy, the softest dynamic marking in the piece is saved for this one exquisite final chord.

"You Have Merely to Listen"

Debussy's most famous quotation reads, "Some people wish above all to conform to the rules, I wish only to render what I can hear. . . . There is no theory. You have merely to listen. Pleasure is the law." Though the part of this quotation that has generally received the most attention has been the idea of freeing oneself from all rules and theory in favor of anarchic pleasure, Debussy's use of the word "merely" is equally interesting. "You have *merely* to listen." Debussy's remarkable aesthetic depended on a kind of sensitivity and listening that was anything but "merely." His compositional language responded with a kind of heightened awareness to every musical stimulus—a leap, a melodic fragment, a chord, or a rhythm—and his universe in which "less is more" and "even less is even more" can help us learn to listen for the nuanced spectrum of grays that always lies hidden beneath black and white. In Debussy's world, everything has the potential for beauty. Even two simple footsteps in the snow.

Debussy's words "you have merely to listen" could well serve as an epigraph for this book. As I mentioned in the introduction, listening, not reading, is ultimately the point of this book. The words of the text in the end are nothing but pointers toward musical sounds that I hope you will now notice in a new way. If you have worked your way through the book's examples and Web site carefully, you should now "own" eighteen pieces of music in a deeply satisfying way. I hope that these pieces will serve as a point of entry not only to other works by these eighteen composers but also to music by the many other wonderful composers I was unable to include in the book. Composition, of course, did not stop with Debussy, and though a discussion of the rich diversity of twentieth- and twenty-first-century music would require a book of its own (which I plan someday to write), I hope that you will begin to explore this repertoire as well. The new sounds, rhythms, and vocabularies that this music contains can seem bewildering at first; however, the way that today's composers work with musical ideas is not nearly as different from that of the composers in this book as you might suspect. Any encounter with a piece of music, old or new, is an encounter with a unique expressive world that has its own individual vocabulary, grammar, and style of speech. It is my deepest belief that if you spend time with any great piece of music, old or new, it will teach you its language. As Debussy said, "You have merely to listen."

GLOSSARY

accidental A note outside the given key. For example, in the key of C major (all white keys on the piano), any sharp or flat (any black-key note).

antecedent phrase The first phrase in a pair of musical phrases that complement each other and stand in the relationship of question and answer. (The second phrase is called the consequent phrase.)

arpeggio From the Italian *arpeggiare*, meaning "to play the harp." Playing the notes of a chord one at a time instead of simultaneously.

cadenza A passage of display in a concerto, generally toward the end of a movement, where the soloist plays alone to show his virtuosity.

canon A piece of music in which multiple voices enter one after the other, singing or playing the same melody. Like a round (e.g., "Row, Row, Row Your Boat").

chromatic scale A scale that moves up or down by half steps—the smallest interval on the piano. Each note in a chromatic scale moves to the next nearest black or white note on the piano.

coda A final concluding section of a piece of music that brings it to a convincing close.

diminished chord A chord of three notes, all a minor third (three half steps) apart. For example, B, D, F.

dominant chord A major triad built on the fifth degree of a major or minor scale. In the key of C, the chord G, B, D. ("The" of "The End.")

dominant-seventh chord A dominant chord with a seventh added. In the key of C, the chord G, B, D, F.

fermata A symbol telling the performer to hold a note or a rest longer than its written value. From the Italian *fermare*, meaning "to stop" or "to dwell on."

grace note A short, ornamental note played quickly before the principal note. In printed music, grace notes are written in smaller type to indicate their ornamental nature.

invertible counterpoint A technique often used in a contrapuntal piece (or passage) of music in which the top part can become the bottom part and vice versa. A procedure in which the parts are "flipped upside down," or inverted.

octave An interval of seven half steps. The octave is the most perfect of all consonances, with a frequency ratio of 2:1. Notes that are an octave apart (e.g., middle C on the piano and the C an octave higher) give the impression of being the same note.

opera seria A type of eighteenth-century opera based on a serious plot as opposed to comic opera or opera buffa. Mozart's *Idomeneo* is an example of opera seria, whereas *The Marriage of Figaro* is an example of opera buffa.

pedal point A held or repeated note—usually in the bass—above which the upper parts change. Imagine an organist holding down a single note with a foot pedal throughout an entire passage.

recapitulation The final section of a movement in sonata form in which the materials of the exposition return, transposed to the home key and resolved.

recitative A style of vocal writing designed to imitate conversational speech often used in opera for narrative dialogue.

reharmonization Repeating a melody or motive while changing the chords underneath.

retransition In a sonata-form movement, the final portion of the development section that leads to the return of the main theme.

ritornello From the Italian meaning "little return." A passage that returns throughout a piece of music in literal or varied form. For example, the opening orchestral section of a Baroque concerto, or an instrumental interlude between the verses of a song or an aria.

tenth An interval of fifteen (minor tenth) or sixteen (major tenth) half steps. The same distance as a third (e.g., from C to E-flat or E) plus an octave.

theme group A group of connected themes that combine to form a larger section of music. For example, the "first theme group" of a sonata-form exposition refers to all of the themes in the home key before the music arrives at a second key.

third An interval of three (minor third) or four (major third) half steps. For example, from C to E-flat or from C to E.

tonic chord The chord built on the home note of a given key. In the key of C major, a C-major chord is the tonic chord.

transpose To repeat a musical idea beginning on a different note.

turn A musical ornament of four or five notes that "turns" around—that is, decorates—a given note by alternating the main note with the notes above it and below it. For example, if C is the main note, a typical four-note turn figure might be D–**C**–B–**C** and a typical five-note turn figure might be **C**–D–**C**–B–**C**.

tutti Italian for "all." In orchestral music, an indication that a passage is to be played by the whole orchestra as opposed to by the soloists. In Baroque concertos, a designation for sections in which the soloist(s) play(s) in unison with the full ensemble.

voice leading The way the various voice parts move.

INDEX